D1475051

God and the Victim

ACADEMY SERIES

SERIES EDITOR
Kimberly Rae Connor, University of San Francisco

A Publication Series of

The American Academy of Religion
and
Oxford University Press

THE SPECTER OF SPECIESISM
Buddhist and Christian Views of Animals
Paul Waldau

INCARNATION AND PHYSICS
Natural Science in the Theology of Thomas F. Torrance
Tapio Luoma

OF BORDERS AND MARGINS
Hispanic Disciples in Texas, 1888–1945
Daisy L. Machado

YVES CONGAR'S THEOLOGY OF THE HOLY SPIRIT
Elizabeth Teresa Groppe

HSIEH LIANG-TSO AND THE *ANALECTS* OF CONFUCIUS
Humane Learning as a Religious Quest
Thomas W. Selover

GREGORY OF NYSSA AND THE CONCEPT OF DIVINE PERSONS
Lucian Turcescu

GRAHAM GREENE'S CATHOLIC IMAGINATION
Mark Bosco, S.J.

COMING TO THE EDGE OF THE CIRCLE
A Wiccan Initiation Ritual
Nikki Bado-Fralick

THE ETHICS OF ANIMAL EXPERIMENTATION
A Critical Analysis and Constructive Christian Proposal
Donna Yarri

PAUL IN ISRAEL'S STORY
Self and Community at the Cross
John L. Meech

CROSSING THE ETHNIC DIVIDE
The Multiethnic Church on a Mission
Kathleen Garces-Foley

GOD AND THE VICTIM
Traumatic Intrusions on Grace and Freedom
Jennifer Erin Beste

AAR

God and the Victim

Traumatic Intrusions
on Grace and Freedom

JENNIFER ERIN BESTE

2007

OXFORD
UNIVERSITY PRESS

Oxford University Press, Inc., publishes works that further
Oxford University's objective of excellence
in research, scholarship, and education.

Oxford New York
Auckland Cape Town Dar es Salaam Hong Kong Karachi
Kuala Lumpur Madrid Melbourne Mexico City Nairobi
New Delhi Shanghai Taipei Toronto

With offices in
Argentina Austria Brazil Chile Czech Republic France Greece
Guatemala Hungary Italy Japan Poland Portugal Singapore
South Korea Switzerland Thailand Turkey Ukraine Vietnam

Published by Oxford University Press, Inc.
198 Madison Avenue, New York, New York 10016

www.oup.com

Sections of chapter 4 (treatment of Butler) were first published
as "The Limits of Poststructuralism for Feminist Theology,"
Journal of Feminist Studies in Religion, v. 22.1 (Spring 2006): 5–19.

Ideas and sections of the manuscript first appeared in "Receiving
and Responding to God's Grace: A Re-Examination in Light
of Trauma Theory." *Journal of the Society of Christian Ethics*
(23:1, Spring/Summer 2003:3–20).

The majority of chapter 6 has been reprinted by permission of Sage Publications Ltd.
"Recovery from Sexual Violence and Socially Mediated Dimensions
of God's Grace: Implications for Christian Communities," by Jennifer Beste
in *Studies in Christian Ethics* 18:2, pp. 89–112, Sage Publications 2005.

Library of Congress Cataloging-in-Publication Data
Beste, Jennifer Erin.
God and the victim : traumatic intrusions on grace and freedom / Jennifer Erin Beste.
p. cm.—(American Academy of Religion academy series)
Includes bibliographical references and index.
ISBN 978-0-19-531109-9
1. Christianity—Psychology. 2. Post-traumatic stress disorder—Religious aspects—Christianity.
3. Grace (Theology). 4. Salvation—Christianity. 5. Liberty—Religious aspects—Christianity.
I. Title.
BR110.B47 2007
233'.7—dc22 2006037211

9 8 7 6 5 4 3 2 1

Printed in the United States of America
on acid-free paper

For my parents, Joseph and Janice Beste, for their unfailing support.

And for "Lauren," whose daily courage and strength in confronting her abusive past are a profound witness to God's and others' love. Her spirit is truly inspiring, and I thank her for her friendship.

Acknowledgments

Throughout graduate school and particularly while writing this book, I learned that supportive relationships are not just essential for recovery from trauma; they are also crucial for sustaining one through the trials of the writing process. I thank my dissertation advisor, Margaret Farley, whose consistent encouragement helped me persist through moments of doubt and whose constructive insights improved my writing immensely. Thanks also to my dissertation co-advisor, Serene Jones, for her enthusiastic support of my work and for her willingness to meet weekly and discuss trauma and theology during a two-year reading course. Next, I am grateful to Gene Outka, whose work on interpersonal harm and whose guidance during the beginning stages of this project were invaluable. Thomas Ogletree also has my deep appreciation for his kind support and willingness to discuss relevant theological concerns. By no means least, I also thank my friends Susan Pfeil, Cyndi Hess, and Shelly Rambo, who spent time with me wrestling with the theological concerns raised by trauma. Furthermore, friendships with my ethics colleagues at Yale, which contributed to my own growth and overall quality of my manuscript, constitute one of the real highlights of my doctoral work.

I also wish to express gratitude to my wonderful colleagues at Xavier University, especially to Father Ken Overberg, S.J., for his feedback on a key section of the manuscript. Thanks also go to Kimberly Connor of the University of San Francisco, editor of the American

Academy of Religion Academy Series, and Cynthia Read, Executive Editor at Oxford University Press.

Finally, I gratefully acknowledge my indebtedness to my family. I thank my parents for their wonderful love and support through my many years as a student. I am incredibly grateful to my husband, Steve, for his unfailing sense of humor, enthusiasm for my project, and meticulous reading of chapter drafts. The birth of my daughter, Anna, midway through my dissertation and then the birth of my son, Jamison, during its revising process were incredible blessings; their mischievous smiles and laughter helped to balance me when I felt weighted down by the reality of traumatic abuse.

Finally, words cannot convey my appreciation to "Lauren," an incest survivor willing to be interviewed repeatedly over a span of several years. Our conversations deepened my passion for exploring the ways in which Christian theology and ethics can most adequately attend to trauma survivors.

Contents

God and the Victim

I

Challenges of Interpersonal Harm for a Theology of Freedom and Grace

I never imagined as a fourteen-year-old growing up in Minnesota that there was a two-year-old girl named Audrey in Tennessee who was about to be raped for the first time by a man that her mother, a prostitute, had brought home. At the time, my own worst fear was striking out yet again in front of peers on my softball team. I survived, of course, and seven years later, as Audrey's sexual abuse finally ended, I was thoroughly enjoying college. Eventually our paths crossed: Audrey, following her third suicide attempt at age eleven, had landed in the same psychiatric hospital where I, an MDiv student at Vanderbilt Divinity School, was working part time as a mental health care intern. On the day we met, Audrey shared the advice that she never had the chance to follow herself: "Never let a man take sexual advantage of you."

During the next two years at this hospital, although I met many sexually abused children and adolescents, there was something about Audrey that disturbed me the most. Something I couldn't quite put my finger on left me disoriented for hours after each shift. Audrey never seemed to interact directly with anyone. Preferring to sing to herself, the blond-haired eleven-year-old with piercing green eyes had a dreamy and whimsical demeanor, an image I could never quite reconcile with her bandaged wrists. During reports of each patient at the beginning of my shifts, many of the staff would describe Audrey as pathetic and hopeless.

I asked her psychiatrists and counselors, "Can't more be done for Audrey? What's really in store for her? Is there any hope she'll recover from so many years of abuse?" To the dismay of a young, idealistic student looking for justice and healing, one counselor answered regretfully but unequivocally, "No, the damage done to that child is too severe. She'll never achieve the kind of psychological functioning that you and I take for granted every day." Her psychiatrist remarked, "With the way insurance is these days, we only have time to put a bandage on all of her problems and discharge her as soon as she's not an imminent suicide threat. We have no time to address the root of the problem."

Encounters with Audrey and other abused children troubled me greatly and frequently disrupted my "other life" as a divinity student, for they assaulted my most cherished beliefs about human freedom and God's goodness. The "truth" of common Christian refrains I'd heard all my life such as "God never gives us more than we can handle" and "Everything happens for a reason" began to evaporate during those years. In a paper for one of my theology classes, I reflected on my work at the psychiatric hospital and asked, "Do these kids really have the freedom to overcome their self-destructive actions and cultivate healthy relationships with themselves and others? How can a God who is truly loving allow these kids to be subject to such human cruelty and be so damaged? How can we honestly have faith in the power of God's grace when confronted with the suffering of these kids?"

I don't know whether Audrey managed to survive the next five years; if she did, she would have turned sixteen during the time I found myself immersed in the more manageable world of a theological ethics doctoral program. Furiously writing a comprehensive exam defending Karl Rahner's formulation of the fundamental option,[1] I was personally gripped by Rahner's empowering narrative of a loving God whose grace enables each person the freedom for self-determination. According to Rahner, grace enables us to freely choose whether we say yes or no to God's offer of communion with the divine by dedicating ourselves to loving our neighbor. After a brief moment of elation as I finished my defense of Rahner, I suddenly was struck with memories of Audrey and my prior questions regarding freedom, grace, and the goodness of God.

During the next few years, extensive research on the effects of child sexual abuse led me into the broader area of contemporary trauma theory, which concerns itself with the vast array of traumatic events and their impact on individuals, families, communities, and cultures. Interestingly, soldiers, civilians subject to war, witnesses to brutal acts of violence and genocide, and victims of domestic and sexual violence often share similar physiological, psychological, and behavioral responses. This book represents my sustained attempt to address the challenges that sexual abuse and other traumas pose for cherished theological beliefs about human possibilities for ourselves as we try to grow personally and love God and neighbor. In the end, I seek to offer a credible Christian account of freedom and grace that does not blind Christians to persons' vulnerability to severe interpersonal harm but that empowers trauma survivors in their process of recovery and invites Christian communities to rethink what it means to love one's neighbor.

Defining Trauma and Its Impact

What exactly is trauma? Although there is no universally accepted definition, trauma is generally understood as a state of being negatively overwhelmed, both physically and psychologically: it is the experience of terror, loss of control, and utter helplessness during a stressful event that threatens one's physical and/or psychological integrity. The especially sinister side of trauma is that, even when the event has ended, it has only begun to shatter one's key assumptions about oneself and one's relations to others in the world. Severe trauma destroys a sense of self-protection, personal invulnerability, and safety in a world that has lost all predictability. The disintegration of one's perception of self and world disrupts one's normal pattern of functioning. In worst-case scenarios, trauma victims are compelled to take their lives, a phenomenon more common than is publicly acknowledged.

After a traumatic event, almost all persons experience intense emotional distress and frequent memory intrusions of the trauma as they struggle emotionally and cognitively to adjust their sense of reality. For some relatively lucky individuals, being preoccupied with the traumatic event gradually allows them to integrate it into their life story and to view it as a painful past experience.[2]

While such persons are able to recover from the traumatic experience and return to a psychologically healthy state of functioning, others remain, due to complex factors, overwhelmed long beyond the acute phase of a traumatic event. Instead of experiencing a gradual decrease in the intensity of emotions and memories surrounding the trauma, these individuals reexperience the traumatic memories as though the original traumatic event were presently occurring.[3] Subsequently, they develop a host of physiological, affective, cognitive, and behavioral responses now identified as posttraumatic stress disorder (PTSD) symptoms. Bessel van der Kolk, a leading trauma theorist, notes that the inability to integrate the traumatic event into one's understanding of reality results in a "repetitive replaying of the trauma in images, behaviors, feelings, physiological states, and interpersonal relationships."[4]

An enduring key issue for those who study trauma is the role a traumatic event plays in the process of becoming traumatized: does the etiology of traumatization lie more in the severity and nature of the event itself or in the traumatized individual's personality, coping style, and psychological/biological vulnerabilities? Why is it that some persons recover from trauma while others experience intrusive traumatic memories and develop multiple PTSD symptoms—symptoms that often cause dramatic personality changes, disruptions in interpersonal relationships and careers, and an overall decline in psychological functioning?

Historically, psychiatric professionals—in line with the prevailing cultural mindset of Western societies—have answered such questions about the etiology of trauma by blaming its effects on the psychological/biological vulnerabilities and/or moral weaknesses of the individual trauma victim. For instance, women who suffered from "hysteria" in the nineteenth century were berated as malingerers or were considered to be simply insane. Likewise, soldiers in the First and Second World Wars who manifested posttraumatic stress symptoms and lost the ability to function in combat were regarded with contempt and accused of cowardice and moral weakness.[5]

What lies behind our societal impulse to blame traumatized individuals for their suffering? Van der Kolk suggests that doing otherwise would threaten our cherished conceptions that the world is essentially just and that persons are free, self-determining individuals responsible for their destiny:

> Society becomes resentful about having its illusions of safety and predictability ruffled by people who remind them of how fragile security can be. . . . Society's reactions [to traumatized people] seems to be primarily conservative impulses in the service of maintaining the beliefs that the world is fundamentally just, that people can be in charge of their lives, and that bad things only happen to people who deserve them.[6]

Since 1980, when PTSD first became an official psychiatric diagnosis, significant worldwide research has been conducted on the impact of different kinds of trauma on individual persons, families, communities, and societies as a whole. By undermining the rationale for blaming the individual, however, many of these studies indicate there is no simple way to determine why some persons recover from traumatic events while others develop PTSD. Findings suggest that the degree to which an event will overwhelm and traumatize a person depends on an interrelation among many complex factors. In general, these factors fall into four categories.[7] First to influence one's response is the nature of the trauma—its kind, severity, frequency, and duration. Second, factors related to the individual trauma victim influence the likelihood of developing PTSD. These factors are "givens"—for example, biological traits, genetic vulnerability to overwhelming stress, psychiatric risk factors, the effect of trauma on one's central nervous system, past experiences, the developmental level of the person when the trauma occurs, and the strength of one's psychological defenses and sense of self prior to the trauma. Third, family dynamics and the quality of support on familial and social levels affect how an individual is able to recover from a traumatic event. When trauma is cloaked in secrecy, for example, its harmful effects inevitably increase as the person becomes more and more isolated from external social support that would help restore a sense of safety and protection. As van der Kolk argues,

> External validation about the reality of a traumatic experience in a safe and supportive context is a vital aspect of preventing and treating post-traumatic stress. . . . When the meaning of trauma is secret, forbidden, or unacceptable . . . trauma is unlikely to result in the mobilization of external resources, in restitution, or in the meting out of justice. Because of the lack of validation and support, traumatic memories are more likely to continue to prey on the victims' minds, and to be expressed as anger, withdrawal, or otherwise disrupted and disrupting behaviors.[8]

Fourth, the broader cultural, social, and political context in which trauma occurs either facilitates or impedes individual persons' capacity to cope with and recover from trauma. Recently, a growing number of social scientists have argued that more attention needs to be focused on the role of cultural and social factors in either preventing or exacerbating conditions that contribute to the onset of PTSD:

> Traumatic experience needs to be conceptualized in terms of a dynamic, two-way interaction between the victimized individual and the surrounding society, evolving over time, and not only as a relatively static, circumscribable entity to be located and addressed within the individual psychology of those affected. . . . Post traumatic symptoms are not just a private and individual problem but also an indictment of the social contexts which produced them.[9]

Some theorists suggest that social injustices like racism and poverty constitute in themselves a distinct form of chronic trauma that contributes significantly to the onset of PTSD.[10]

Overall, research findings suggest that blaming victims for posttraumatic symptoms is not only erroneous but also contributes to the vicious cycle of traumatization. An adequate understanding of human freedom must take seriously the research studies demonstrating that none of these four factors has to do with the free choice or moral character of trauma victims. Our attempts to understand the experience of severe traumatization, therefore, bring us very quickly to questions of human vulnerability and human freedom. Indeed, recent developments in trauma theory challenge longstanding assumptions in Western liberal theory about the self as a free agent. But the challenge goes even further, all the way to religious and theological convictions about the self and one's freedom and responsibility before God. To address these latter challenges, it is necessary not only to take trauma theory seriously but also to probe the ongoing credibility of theological anthropologies that place human freedom at their center.

Trauma's Challenge to the Christian Tradition

Confronting our human vulnerability to traumatization and recognizing the strong social impulses to deny such vulnerability challenges not only the Western liberal self, who is supposed to be freely self-determining, but also significant beliefs within the Christian tradition. There are many ways that severe trauma impacts the self and agency and challenges theological convictions concerning the relation between the self, human freedom, and divine grace. Overall, the Christian tradition has held that a person's capacity to respond to God's grace by loving both God and neighbor is not entirely vulnerable to earthly contingencies: interpersonal harms, however severe, cannot separate one from the grace of God and from the power to love others and live well.

One prominent strand in the Christian tradition, represented by theologians such as St. Augustine (in his early writings), Thomas Aquinas, Søren Kierkegaard, and Karl Rahner, has held specifically that, with the aid of God's grace, persons have both the freedom and responsibility to respond to God's grace and become morally virtuous persons who love God and love their neighbor as themselves. For instance, although Aquinas acknowledges that good and ill fortune befall humans in different proportions and can affect temporal happiness, he nevertheless affirms that God gives persons sufficient temporal goods to become virtuous persons.[11] Furthermore, he argues that interpersonal harm cannot ultimately harm us spiritually: "No man can of himself be sufficient cause of another's spiritual death, because no man dies spiritually except by sinning of his own will."[12] More adamantly, Kierkegaard claims that persons are equal in their ability to accept God's grace and give themselves completely to God:

> I cannot abandon the thought that every man, absolutely every man, however simple he is, however much he may suffer, can nevertheless grasp the highest, namely religion, I cannot forget that. If that is not so, then Christianity is really nonsense . . . and I can't be bothered to live.[13]

In the twentieth century, Karl Rahner generally echoes these convictions of Aquinas and Kierkegaard when he affirms that every person, with the aid of God's grace, is confronted with the inescapable task to respond in freedom, positively or negatively, to God's self-communication. For Rahner and many other Christians, this response is at the heart of what it means to be a human being.

Another major strand in the Christian tradition, represented by the later Augustine, Martin Luther, John Calvin, and Karl Barth, seems to repudiate any significant role for free choice in one's love for others and response to God's salvific action. Nonetheless, even these theologians vehemently deny that the capacity for love of God and neighbor is wholly vulnerable to interpersonal harm. Since Christian faith and salvation stem from God's unmerited grace, no external harms can interfere with the sovereign power of such grace to justify and sanctify an individual and enable him or her to love God and others.

The belief, then, that our ability (whether by freedom and/or grace) to respond to God's grace is not entirely vulnerable to earthly contingencies is firmly embedded in the Christian tradition. Does this longstanding, widespread conviction, however, remain credible in light of recent social scientific research on the insidious effects of severe, interpersonal injury to traumatized persons' identities and freedom? Should we not consider more carefully the possibility that we can harm one another to such an extent that someone's capacity to respond to God's grace can be severely diminished, if not altogether destroyed? Entirely different issues and complexities arise, depending on whether one affirms a role for human freedom in one's response to God's grace. In this book, I confine myself to considering how trauma theory challenges the strand of Christian tradition that affirms a necessary role for freedom in one's eternal destiny of salvation. In short, the question is this: if the heart of salvation includes a free response to God, and if severe trauma can make this impossible, what does this mean for theological anthropology—for our understanding of what it means to be a person called to say yes to God's self-offer? The challenges posed by trauma theory to theologians who already hold a different view of theological anthropology and the way to salvation, that is, who believe that God's unmerited grace alone ensures a person's acceptance of God's offer of salvation, will need to be explored in a separate work.[14]

The unique orientation and overall contribution of this book is best understood against the backdrop of the work of key contemporary theologians and ethicists who have approached similar questions about interpersonal harm and freedom.[15] In his article "On Harming Others," Gene Outka asks to what degree persons can harm and help one another morally and religiously. He asks: "What limits, if any, are set to the harm others can do to us or we to them?"[16] Outka is particularly concerned whether interpersonal harm has the power to corrupt a person's will entirely or destroy an individual's relation to God through no fault of his or her own: "Can someone else take my soul from me, or do I alone have the power to lose it?"[17] Essentially, Outka wrestles with whether an individual's eternal destiny of damnation could be solely determined by unfortunate contingencies in temporal life like severe, interpersonal harm. He mines both scripture and tradition for grounds to conclude that persons are neither wholly invulnerable to interpersonal harm nor wholly vulnerable. He therefore denies that persons can be damned through no moral fault of their own; when a victim incurs ultimate religious harm (damnation), both violator and victim share coresponsibility in the event.

In his article "Arminian Edification: Kierkegaard on Grace and Free Will," Timothy Jackson concurs with Outka that we cannot harm one another to such an extreme that someone can necessitate another's moral corruption and/or damnation without any fault at all on the part of the other. Unlike Outka, however, Jackson claims that we may harm a person to such an extent that we permanently thwart his or her ability to commit an initial free act and thus become a moral agent at all: "Abuses of freedom, including the perversion or loss of freedom, may always be by one's own hand, but the failure ever to acquire freedom may be due to outside interference."[18] Appealing to cases of severe child abuse and torture, Jackson asserts, "We can suspend others in an impersonal limbo, if you will, by victimizing them into moral oblivion."[19] He argues that, while this kind of harm is not ultimate in the sense that such persons will be damned (since damnation presupposes moral agency and responsibility), it is still a profound harm, since it robs persons of the possibility of freedom to accept God's grace.

The philosopher/theologian Simone Weil and feminist theologians like Dorothee Soelle, Wendy Farley, and Marjorie Suchocki also wrestle in their theological analyses of suffering and violence with the degree to which persons can harm one another. With the exception of Suchocki, each of these theologians appears to affirm the possibility that human freedom can be completely destroyed by extreme forms of interpersonal harm. The kind of suffering they describe is not limited to, but includes, the suffering that results from trauma inflicted by other persons. In fact, their depictions of extreme suffering bear striking resemblance to contemporary depictions of the dynamics involved in traumatization.[20]

Simone Weil describes an event as constituting affliction if it has uprooted and attacked a human life in all dimensions: physically, psychologically, and socially.[21] Since affliction involves "social degradation or the fear of it in some form," it can be argued that one of the factors involved in the onset of affliction includes some form of interpersonal neglect or harm. If persons were offered sufficient social support, they presumably would be spared from the radical suffering that constitutes affliction. Weil characterizes a person who is afflicted as "a being struggling like a half-crushed worm," rendered incapable of even expressing the sense of mutilation he or she is experiencing.[22]

In her appropriation of Weil's depiction of affliction, Soelle argues that some persons "are so thoroughly destroyed through continual suffering that they can respond only in helpless or aggressive attempts to flee."[23] Such extreme suffering leads to despair and paralysis in every meaningful dimension of human existence:

> There is pain that renders people blind and deaf. Feeling for others dies; suffering isolates the person and he no longer cares about anyone but himself. . . . Extreme suffering turns a person in on himself completely. It destroys his ability to communicate.[24]

Farley refers to this form of suffering as "radical" and describes it as undeserved and "destructive of the human spirit."[25] She claims that radical suffering attacks those abilities that make persons most human: the capacities to "exercise freedom to feel affection, to hope, to love God."[26] Such suffering has the power to destroy innocent or "passionately good" persons, crippling their spirit so decisively that they can no longer defy evil: "Spirits can be destroyed just as bones can be broken and bodies killed. Human beings can be subjected to such pain that they are crushed rather than redeemed by it."[27]

Echoing the findings of trauma research, Weil, Soelle, and Farley argue that victims of radical suffering not only are unable to defy evil, but they also participate in their own self-destruction. Weil describes affliction as stamping one's soul like a red-hot iron with self-hatred, defilement, and guilt that causes one to act self-destructively.[28] Farley argues that victims of radical suffering are not morally culpable for such self-destructive acts:

> The sign of radical suffering is that the person is made inhuman by suffering. But the complicity of the self in its own destruction does not parallel the culpability of sin. The absence of even the desire for freedom from pain makes plain the hideous damage that suffering

> can do to the human spirit. Persons who are so badly hurt that they become accomplices in their own destruction, far from sharing responsibility for their defeat, are persons already broken by pain. Part of the terrible guilt borne by the victimizer lies in cruelty's power not only to hurt people but literally to destroy them.[29]

In her work *The Fall to Violence*, although Marjorie Suchocki appears to share Farley's conviction that radical suffering has the power to turn a person against himself or herself, she does not finally claim that persons are inevitably crushed by such events. True to her process metaphysics, Suchocki maintains that it is always possible for a victim to transcend the violence; freedom, then, is never completely destroyed:

> Traumatic violations have the power to overwhelm not only the past, but the present as well, interfering with normal selectivity. But no moment, no matter how traumatic, can of itself crowd out the novelty of the future. Every moment contains a potential for novelty that can break the grip of the past. When, then, one experiences the continuation in the present of a past violation, the past alone is not sufficient to account for that continuation. There is a sense, however small, in which the victim is also involved in maintaining the vitality of that violation through its continuation in the present. . . . A degree of novelty and freedom, even if minute, is inescapably a part of every moment, and it can be sufficient to break the continuity of violence. One can will one's well-being.[30]

Suchocki, like Outka, thus appears to embrace the idea that, when moral loss is involved, it must be that violator and victim are coresponsible for the resulting harms.

How are we to adjudicate between these contemporary theologians' conflicting views of the impact of interpersonal harm on human freedom? Were Aquinas, Kierkegaard, and Rahner insensitive or blind to the extent to which persons are vulnerable to earthly contingencies, or are certain contemporary theologians exaggerating the scope of the effects of interpersonal harm? Do trauma victims share coresponsibility for self-destructive acts, or has interpersonal harm deprived them of moral agency and responsibility?

Jackson, Soelle, and Farley assert that we can destroy one another's ability to act freely and relate positively to God. However, not one of these thinkers goes to any great lengths to establish such a serious claim—a claim that has vast theological and moral ramifications. For if these theologians' descriptions of the effects of interpersonal harm are accurate, they call into question many key Christian beliefs about the nature of God, the relation between divine grace and human freedom, the meaning of sin, and the development of any adequate theodicy.

This book attempts to press these sorts of issues in new ways. The main contribution I wish to make is to articulate a credible theology of freedom and grace that adequately attends to the experiences of severely traumatized persons. This involves critical scrutiny of the insistence in most theologies of freedom that persons' freedom for ultimate self-disposition with the aid of grace is not entirely vulnerable to earthly contingencies. Since it is beyond the scope of this book to examine all theologies of freedom in the context of trauma theory, I have chosen to focus on Karl Rahner's theology of freedom as a paradigmatic example for several reasons.[31]

First, it is difficult to underestimate Rahner's influence on contemporary theology and ethics, especially on Roman Catholic theology: Rahner's formulation of freedom as a fundamental option is one of the most well-known theologies of freedom in the twentieth century. If it turns out that his account of grace and freedom is inadequate in the context of trauma, contemporary theology that relies on presumptions embedded in his theological anthropology will likewise need to be reexamined.

Second, Rahner's theological and ethical method views human experiences as a valid resource for interpreting the truth and content of theological doctrines. Rahner consistently seeks to relate revelation to concrete human experience and contemporary self-understanding. Typically, he likes to show relevant "connections by correspondence."[32] According to Rahner, one of the central tasks of theology involves demonstrating how a person, on reflection, could perceive how each theological doctrine expresses something true about his or her existence. Reflecting on theological assertions about the human person, for example, Rahner says that everyone should be able to "recognize himself as that person who is here trying to express his self-understanding, or whether in responsibility to himself and to his existence he can affirm as the conviction which is to be the truth for him that he is not such a person as Christianity tells him he is."[33]

This leads to a third reason that Rahner's theology is particularly apt for the task of this book. Since he recognizes the complexity of interpreting human experience in light of revelation, Rahner argues for the need to incorporate insights from the physical and social sciences when attempting to elucidate theological doctrines. He writes, "Theology has itself directly to turn its attention to the natural sciences, inquiring into their basic outlook and their autonomy, and allowing itself to be conditioned by them.... The same must be said about the relationship between social sciences and theology."[34] Appropriating insights from the social sciences, Rahner shares contemporary concerns about taking seriously the historicity and sociality of the human condition when defending his account of radical freedom. Given all of these commitments present in his theological method, Rahner's theology of freedom is among the best candidates to accommodate a full range of human experiences, including severe traumatic experiences.

The focus of this book is to examine the challenges trauma theory raises to Rahner's theology of freedom. With the help of trauma studies and insights from feminist theory, I seek to revise his theology to respond successfully to such challenges. I argue that a revised theology of freedom needs to acknowledge the possibility that interpersonal harm has the power to destroy a person's capacity to realize sufficient freedom to love self, neighbor, and God.[35] In turn, confronting this possibility raises questions about grace and its relation to human freedom. For this reason, developing a theology of freedom that speaks to the experiences of traumatized persons requires me to grapple, in greater depth than the aforementioned authors, with how to understand the workings of grace in light of the intense despair and utter brokenness that often result from severe interpersonal harm. Simone Weil is the only thinker I have discussed who explicitly struggles with God's allowing such affliction: "It is surprising that God should have given affliction the power to seize the very souls of the innocent and to take possession of them as their sovereign lord."[36] Weil ultimately claims that God's grace does not have the power to "cure the irremediably wounded nature here below."[37] My own analysis of the power of God's grace to foster healing is more hopeful than Weil's. Drawing on trauma survivors' experiences of recovery from traumatization, I suggest that a crucial way in which God mediates grace to remedy this harm is through the indirect means of interpersonal, loving relationships. Thus, I argue that survivors' experiences of both interpersonal harm and support offer crucial insights leading to a more adequate understanding of the relation between God's grace and human freedom. Ultimately, such insights result in ethical implications that significantly challenge Christian communities' perceptions of what it means to love one's neighbor.

The following anticipatory summary of the chapters introduces more specifically the questions I pose, and the way my responses develop and unfold. In chapter 2, I draw on Rahner's best known writings in *Theological Investigations* and *Foundations of Christian Faith* to elucidate his account of the relation between the self, human freedom, and God's grace. Conceiving of God as the ground of all persons' being, Rahner believes that God creates humans as beings who essentially become themselves by responding in freedom to God's self-communication. While Rahner acknowledges that persons are determined to a significant extent by historical, cultural, and biological factors, he nevertheless argues that persons who possess reason ultimately have the transcendental and categorical freedom to realize who they will become before God. Such freedom does not mean merely the choice to do this or that, but the freedom to effect a fundamental option to accept or reject God's self-communication finally and irrevocably. Salvation consists of an interplay between the divine freedom to offer God's self and the human freedom to accept God's self-communication. Rahner argues that persons actualize this transcendental freedom through concrete acts of loving God and neighbor. He generally holds that, although sin makes the choice to overcome egoism and love others "difficult and painful," the free decision to love God and others in and through a fundamental option is always possible.

In chapter 3, I analyze the impact of severe trauma on persons' selfhood, capacity for relationality, and freedom for self-determination. To address the complex effects of trauma on the sense of self and capacity for freedom, I focus on one population of persons exposed to a specific trauma, women survivors who experienced severe incestuous trauma as young girls. Among the physical and psychological consequences of incest are depression, anxiety, chronic and acute somatizing, dissociation, feelings of isolation and alienation, negative self-image and self-esteem, sexual maladjustment, mental illness, attention deficit disorder, confusion of sex with love, extreme dependency, impaired ability to judge the trustworthiness of others, identification with the aggressor, and various phobias. Behavioral manifestations include such self-destructive acts as suicide attempts and self-mutilation, eating disorders, substance abuse, sexual effects ranging from avoidance to compulsive promiscuity, prostitution, and antisocial acting out in the forms of delinquency, truancy, and criminal behavior.[38] Besides the ways incestuous abuse impedes development of selfhood and agency, it also damages survivors' ability to develop trusting, intimate relationships with others and God. Many therapists who work with incest victims report that the majority experience more anger, shame, and feelings of distance toward God than nonabused women. While more research must be conducted to arrive at a fuller understanding of the effects of sexual abuse on one's God-relation, it seems reasonable to take seriously the possibility that incestuous abuse can negatively impede and perhaps destroy a person's ability to relate to God and neighbor with faith, trust, and love.

Before attempting to place Rahner's theology of the fundamental option in dialogue with the experiences of incest survivors, I turn in the next chapter to a third conversation partner: feminist theorists. The purpose of chapter 4 is to examine certain feminist conceptions of self and agency that differ from Rahner's theological anthropology. Since feminist theory has been concerned with ways that varied forms of oppression (a type of interpersonal harm) and violence against women impact women's sense of self and agency, it is important to explore whether feminists shed any light on the dynamics of traumatization and recovery from traumatic violence. Paying particular attention to Judith Butler's and Diana Meyers's accounts of the self and agency, I identify certain insights from feminist theory that resonate with the findings of trauma research. While I do not find these philosophers' accounts of the self and agency fully adequate for a theological account of self, freedom, and God's grace, I signal the need to appropriate certain of their insights for my later task of constructing a revised theology of freedom.

In chapter 5, I argue that the experiences of severely traumatized persons and the insights of feminist theory demonstrate Rahner's failure to acknowledge adequately the effects of relationality and embodiment for one's capacity to realize sufficient freedom to effect a fundamental option. I also find Rahner's general construal of the relation between God's grace and human freedom insufficient when attempting to make sense of the workings of God's grace in the lives of trauma survivors. However, I suggest that, by incorporating insights of feminists and trauma theory and drawing on other aspects of Rahner's theology, it is possible to construct a more adequate Rahnerian theology of freedom and grace. I highlight two passages in Rahner's writings that, however brief, appear to waver from his general position that human responsiveness to grace is not wholly vulnerable to interpersonal harm. In this chapter, I argue that a revised account must (1) acknowledge to a greater degree the power of sin against one's neighbor to disable that neighbor's freedom to respond to God's grace, and (2) articulate how God's grace is mediated through loving, interpersonal relations.

Finally, in chapter 6 I explore the ethical implications resulting from this revised understanding of the self, freedom, and God's grace—implications that are relevant to trauma survivors and to Christian communities as a whole. Suggesting that my revised theology of freedom and grace intensifies our sense of collective responsibility for enabling one another's freedom before God, I examine how Christian communities can reach out in love to trauma survivors to nurture healing and recovery from traumatic violence. There is hope that creative acts of neighbor-love can mediate divine grace, fostering incest survivors' freedom to realize their potential to relate lovingly to God and neighbor.

2

Karl Rahner's Theological Anthropology

The Role of Freedom and Grace in the Construction of the Human Self

Before inquiring how experiences of trauma victims challenge certain Christian understandings of the relation between human freedom and God's grace, I begin with Karl Rahner's theology of freedom and grace, which places a capacity for free response to God at the heart of what it means to be a human person. Drawing on central texts in Rahner's *Theological Investigations,* as well as his systematic and more complete treatment of grace and freedom in *Foundations of Christian Faith,* this chapter examines Rahner's theology of freedom and grace. In order to understand the meaning of freedom for Rahner, it is necessary to situate it within his theological anthropology as a whole. Hence, I begin with some general concepts that are important to Rahner and that will set the stage for a consideration of the meaning of freedom. I focus in particular on the existentials that define what it means to be human: transcendence, subjectivity, and radical freedom and responsibility for ultimate self-disposal.[1] I then turn to an exploration of how God's grace is understood to transform human consciousness and destiny, and develop Rahner's full account of human freedom before God.

The Self as Spirit-in-the-World

Person as Transcendent

As early as his first philosophical work, *Spirit in the World*, Rahner begins to develop his philosophical and ultimately theological anthropology, which depicts persons as finite spirits-in-the-world. Rahner characterizes humans as finite spirits who become themselves in and through matter (the world as experienced in space and time). The process of becoming a person and attaining self-awareness and knowledge is dependent on materially encountering the otherness of one's body, other persons, and the rest of creation. Through the power of sensibility, the human spirit receives otherness and becomes immersed in it (*conversio ad phantasm*). Through the power of the intellect, the human spirit returns to itself (*reditio completa*) by objectifying the otherness as finite and distinct from oneself and becoming a self-conscious knower.[2]

Rahner argues that becoming aware of the finitude of one's self, other persons, and the world is crucial for both moving beyond identification with finite objects and consciously preapprehending the existence of an infinite horizon of being. This awareness of an infinite horizon of being, present in every act of knowing, makes possible the human capacity for transcendence. Rahner defines transcendental experience as "the subjective, unthematic, necessary and unfailing consciousness of the knowing subject that is copresent in every spiritual act of knowledge, and the subject's openness to the unlimited expanse of all possible reality."[3]

This transcendental existential of the human condition cannot be objectified; it is manifest in every facet of persons' daily experiences of knowing, desiring, and acting. Persons exhibit a restlessness and resistance toward stasis, along with a dynamism toward further development, that reveal their capacity for transcendence. Since the human spirit is open and boundless, dynamically striving toward the horizon of infinite being, persons are constantly transcending who they presently are as they actualize their potentialities and grow in greater degrees of being. For example, in regard to learning and knowing about themselves and their world, once persons figure out an answer to any kind of question, they immediately ask further questions. They are ultimately able to place everything in question, including the meaning of existence and even themselves in their entirety. Similarly, attaining any kind of temporal goods (material, affective, or intellectual) never fulfills persons permanently; once they have fulfilled one inquiry, desire, or goal, it becomes relativized in importance, and persons are already oriented toward another desire or pursuit. Rahner explicitly maintains that transcendence in this sense is present as an existential in every experience, not only through our knowing but also through our willing and loving.

Rahner acknowledges that, while this transcendental dimension is always present, it is possible and quite easy for persons to fail to attend explicitly to this dimension of their awareness, hence fail to actualize it in its fullness. Persons may feel threatened by the limitlessness of the questions they ask. Turning away from this questioning, many seek to immerse themselves in everyday concerns. They may wish to concentrate their efforts on categorical matters over which they can exercise greater control. Others may evade questions of ultimate significance out of a deep sense of despair that no meaning exists after all.[4] Choosing to turn away from our capacity for self-transcendence is deeply troubling to Rahner, for it undermines our ability to grow and realize greater degrees of fulfillment.

Person as Subject

The human capacity for transcendence is closely linked to subjectivity—another existential that distinguishes human life from other life forms. Humans are subjects who are simultaneously conscious of themselves and capable of objectifying their experiences in the world through acts of transcendence. In his affirmation of subjectivity, Rahner does not deny the extent to which humans are conditioned by externalities such as biological, psychological, and social factors:

> They [these sciences] are all quite legitimately trying to derive and explain man, to dissolve him, as it were, into his empirical causes which can be specified and analyzed and isolated. These sciences are to a large extent correct in their methods and in their results, and everyone's own painful experience in his own existence shows how very right they are.[5]

However, Rahner does not at all view our conditioning as being in tension or opposition with our subjectivity. Rather, as noted, he argues that humans come to know themselves in and through what is other than themselves: "Man experiences himself precisely as subject and person insofar as he becomes conscious of himself as the product of what is radically foreign to him."[6]

Rahner also claims that, despite constant attempts of the empirical sciences to objectify humans and reduce them to particular observable elements, it is impossible to predict how a person, given his set of contingent circumstances, will individuate and mature into the kind of person he ultimately will become. No anthropological theory can account for the totality of a person's self-understanding. According to Rahner, the mere act of persons reflecting on why they have become the way they are reveals that persons experience transcendence and affirm that they are "more than the sum of such analyzable components of [their] reality."[7]

Person as Free and Responsible

Having described persons as aware of themselves in their entirety and able to imagine future possibilities that will shape who they can become, Rahner considers a third existential—freedom and responsibility:

> By the fact that man in his transcendence exists as open and undetermined, he is at the same time responsible for himself. He is left to himself and placed in his own hands not only in his knowledge, but also in his *actions*. It is in being consigned to himself that he experiences himself as responsible and free.[8]

Just as transcendence toward the presence of absolute being ushers in knowledge of ourselves and the world, it also makes possible our transcendental freedom and responsibility. But how can we be confident that transcendence and self-awareness require and make possible such freedom and responsibility? The ability of persons to be self-conscious and conceive of themselves as a totality means that they will inevitably need to respond in some way to their questions and further influence who they are becoming. Rahner argues that persons who assert that they have been completely determined by external factors, hence not responsible for who they have become, have essentially chosen to accept this very interpretation of themselves:

> If someone says that man always experiences himself as determined and controlled from without, as functional and dependent, as able to be analyzed and reduced to antecedents and consequences, the reply must be: the subject who knows this is always at the same time a responsible subject who is challenged to say something and to do something with man's absolute dependence and self-alienation and determination, challenged to take a position on it by either cursing it or accepting it, by being skeptical or by despairing, or whatever. So even when a person would abandon himself into the hands of empirical anthropologies, he still remains in his own hands. He does not

> escape from his freedom, and the only question can be how he interprets himself, and freely interprets himself.[9]

Furthermore, Rahner claims that freedom cannot be viewed in a Christian sense as a neutral capacity to do this or that in an arbitrary order. Such a concept of freedom of choice atomizes the meaning of freedom and reduces it to a freedom of individual, isolated acts. Under this conception of freedom, persons remain neutral in relation to their acts and can always determine themselves anew (in the sense of reversal as well as change) at any time.[10] In contrast, Rahner argues that Christian freedom is self-determining; it involves realizing one's natural tendency toward self-realization and fulfillment. Such freedom is the power to do something definitive, final, and eternal—to actualize or refuse to actualize oneself in one's totality—a task that is achieved over the course of one's entire lifetime.

At this point, an obvious question arises: what constitutes authentic self-realization and how can persons obtain such knowledge? To examine Rahner's response adequately, it is first necessary to turn to his account of God's grace, that is, God's offer of self-communication that transforms human destiny. Only then can one adequately understand what Rahner means by human freedom and self-realization.

God's Gracious Offer of Self-Communication to Humanity

Rahner claims that God's grace in and through Christ's salvific love radically transforms the *telos* of human self-realization and fulfillment. Because God desires to be the Being of absolute nearness and intimate love, God offers Godself through Christ in an intimate self-communication, a gift of grace for all humans: "God wishes to communicate himself, to pour forth the love which he himself is. . . . Everything else exists so that this one thing might be: the eternal miracle of Infinite Love."[11]

According to Rahner, creation and the Incarnation are two moments that signify a unity of the divine desire to offer God's self-communication to humanity.[12] Through the historical events of Christ's death and resurrection, God reveals that the divine commitment and love toward humanity becomes irreversible. Christians can thus trust in God's faithful, abiding love despite the ways in which persons grievously sin and offend God throughout history.

Why does God desire to communicate God's own reality to humanity? Rahner answers that, in this act of graced self-communication, "God becomes a partner in a personal and direct relationship with himself and man," making possible personal and immediate knowledge and love for God.[13] By God's self-communication, Rahner does not mean that God merely reveals something new about the divine being or transforms humanity by giving it some *thing*. Instead, on a more radical level, God freely and gratuitously offers the divine self to each human being: God "does not originally cause and produce something different from himself in the creature, but rather... he communicates his own divine reality and makes it a constitutive element in the fulfillment of the creature."[14] In becoming the constitutive element in the fulfillment of persons, God's gift of self becomes intimately, ontologically present within all persons, orienting them to God transcendentally and dynamically as the absolute being who constitutes their sole fulfillment:

> Grace is a dynamic force which transforms the inner, transcendent reference of the human spirit to God so that this transcendent, spiritual movement finds its fulfillment in the beatific vision, the direct knowledge of God face-to-face and love.... Grace is thus understood as the radical transformation of human transcendence so that God is not merely the final goal of human striving which one may come nearer to but never reach.... Grace is also that which makes it possible for this movement to reach God himself. Naturally, therefore, grace divinizes man and bestows upon him a share in the holiness of God.[15]

Grace as Experienced

In an attempt to convey how God's offer of self-communication is a permanent constitutive element that pervasively manifests itself in every dimension of human existence, Rahner refers to the divine self-communication as a supernatural existential.[16] According to Rahner, this offer, which orients persons to a destiny of communion with God, "gives evidence of itself in human existence and is operative in that existence."[17] Thus, an intimate relationship to God constitutes persons' reality, and everyone experiences grace, although perhaps unreflexively and unthematically. Rahner claims that, like all other transcendental elements present in experience, grace cannot be objectified and isolated from other existents present in daily experience.[18] Instead, grace is copresent and permeates human consciousness, influencing each person's existential experience of what it means to be human. Since grace cannot be objectified, persons cannot know what "pure human nature" is apart from the influence of God's supernatural grace of salvation. As Rahner notes, "Our spiritual transcendence is never merely natural but is always surrounded and carried by a dynamic of grace that points toward God's nearness."[19]

While grace cannot be objectified and identified unambiguously, Rahner does claim that experiences of grace can become thematic on conscious self-reflection. All of our longings and most profound human experiences reflect God's gracious self-communication. In an attempt to heighten persons' explicit awareness of God's grace, Rahner describes situations that most typically manifest the presence of grace, such as forgiving someone who remains thankless, sacrificing something without feeling personal satisfaction, or loving God in spite of doubt and emptiness or when the world seems senseless and absurd.[20] Rahner thus characterizes experiences of grace as transcending egoism, acting selflessly out of love for God, and attaining a sense of meaning that is not limited by the confines of this world.

Acceptance of God's Self-Offer: A Moment of Grace and Human Freedom

Rahner argues that, besides being both Giver and Gift in the divine self-communication, God provides sufficient grace (the condition) that makes possible a human being's act of accepting God's self-communication, the indwelling of God's spirit within the human being. This act of accepting grace, he emphasizes, is itself a graced gift from God.[21] At times, Rahner identifies this grace that empowers human freedom to accept God's offer as created grace. He argues that the divine self-offer (distinguished as uncreated grace)[22] effects positive ontological changes in human consciousness.[23] These transformative effects, called created gifts of grace, elevate and heal human nature, justifying the person and enabling her to transcend her present self and accept God's self-offer: "It is therefore grace itself which sets free our formal freedom in capacity and in act for saving action, and heals it in itself."[24]

This does not mean, however, that grace is irresistible; God's self-communication is presented to each person's human freedom as an offer, and awaits a free human response. When persons respond affirmatively to God's self-offer, they are ratifying God's invitation for a relationship with the divine, which will ultimately culminate in the beatific vision. Grace, then, does not nullify human freedom; rather, it liberates it from the enslaved bondages of original sin and concupiscence, enabling persons to accept freely God's self-communication. Thus, Rahner emphasizes that grace enables a person's freedom to accept God's offer of the divine self—a claim that will be very significant when analyzing the effects of trauma on a person's freedom.

Freedom to Effect a Fundamental Option

There is clearly a great deal at stake in the role of human freedom in Rahner's theology: with the aid of God's grace, persons are capable of freely responding to God's self-communication and becoming partners in an intimate relationship with God that culminates in the future beatific vision. Rahner frequently describes this freedom as the capacity to effect a fundamental option either to accept God's offer of salvation and become the persons God created us to be or reject the divine offer and turn away from our graced, transcendental orientation to God in favor of eternal destruction. Human freedom thus plays a determinative role in the attainment of salvation. Given this immense importance of freedom, it is crucial to examine in greater detail Rahner's analysis of human freedom and what it concretely means to say yes or no to God's self-offer.

As noted, Rahner conceives of human freedom not as the capacity simply to choose among finite objects but as the radical capacity to decide about one's self in one's totality and to choose whether one is good or evil in the very ground of one's being.[25] He insists that persons can never transfer such personal responsibility for self-realization onto others; the very act of renouncing responsibility and blaming others for failure is itself a free decision. He depicts the human self as "lonely and unsheltered, responsible to himself, who can in no way be 'absolved' of the solitary self, who can never throw himself on to others."[26] Becoming good or evil, then, is not a person's accidental condition, derived solely from external influences.[27]

In his analysis of the decision about oneself in one's totality, Rahner distinguishes between transcendental (originating) freedom and categorical (originated) freedom. Transcendental freedom is the power to achieve self-disposal and effect a fundamental option for or against God's self-offer. Such a transcendental yes or no to God cannot remain hidden in an interior disposition but must be mediated and actualized through persons' concrete, historical choices and actions. Rahner refers to these concrete acts of freedom as categorical or originated freedom. He notes: "Man as spirit is not an abstract subject but an embodied, historical spirit who achieves his transcendence precisely by means of the material of the world, of its bodily corporeality and history."[28] Thus, Rahner does not view transcendental and categorical freedom as two separate kinds of freedom but rather as "two moments which form the single unity of freedom."[29]

Rahner argues that, being the temporal and historical beings that they are, persons require time in order to become and to achieve final self-disposal by means of effecting a fundamental option. He rejects the conception of a free subject capable of infinitely revising himself, remaining neutral or unaffected in relation to his actions: "The temporal nature of a personal spirit does not consist of moments which pass away and fall back into the emptiness of what has been; but are rather moments which become in order to exist and remain in the one unified total attitude of the person."[30] Aquinas's insight that our acts leave traces in our being resonates throughout Rahner's reflections about how our present acts shape and circumscribe the range of our future options and decisions. Similarly, our present decisions are codetermined by our previous actions and our present free choice; they then contribute to the ongoing formation of good or bad habits, deeply affecting the very identity of every person and his or her fundamental option for or against God.[31] Temporal decisions, then, determine an individual's final, eternal destiny of either salvation or perdition.[32]

Since we are beings oriented toward God, who is our fulfillment, we ultimately dispose ourselves toward or away from God: "The entire life of the free subject is inevitably an answer to the question in which God offers himself to us as the source of transcendence."[33] Thus, in the process of a person's determining who he wishes to become, he simultaneously effects a fundamental option either to say yes to God's self-offer and actualize himself as God has created him to become or to say no and self-destructively turn away from the source of his being: "This self-realisation is a task he cannot avoid, it is always either a self-realisation in the direction of God or a self-refusal towards God."[34] Each categorical act of freedom, then, affects who one is becoming and simultaneously one's fundamental option toward God. Rahner explains why every categorical action reflects an unthematic "yes" or "no" to God in the following way:

> Freedom takes place as mediated by the concrete world which encounters us, and especially by the world of other persons, even when this freedom intends and wants to be freedom vis-à-vis God immediately and thematically.... Since in every act of freedom which is concerned on the categorical level with a quite definite object, a quite definite person, there is always present, as the condition of possibility for such an act, transcendence towards the absolute terms and source of all our intellectual and spiritual acts, and hence towards God, there can and must be present in every such act an *unthematic "yes" or "no"* to this God of original, transcendental experience.[35]

What, then, constitutes a "yes" or "no" to God's self-communication? According to Rahner, only one human activity ultimately constitutes accepting

God's self-offer: loving God with our whole being. "Love of God," says Rahner, "is the only total integration of human existence."[36] It is the only act in which persons can integrate all of their multifaceted characteristics and desires and attain a sense of wholeness and contentment.

Unity of Love for God and Love for Neighbor

Such love for God, however, cannot exist and be further realized solely in an interior, private disposition between the individual person and God. Rahner claims that our love for God can only be mediated and actualized through loving our neighbor:

> The relationship to God in its directness is necessarily mediated by intramundane communication. . . . The original relationship to God is . . . love of neighbor. If man becomes himself only by the exercise of love towards God and must achieve this self-mastery by a categorical action, then it holds good . . . that the act of love of neighbor is the only categorical and original act in which man attains the whole of the concretely given reality.[37]

Given his conviction that love for neighbor instantiates love for God, Rahner proposes that a unity exists between love of God and love of neighbor.[38] Unity does not mean simply that, by loving one's neighbor, a believer demonstrates obedience to God's commands and thus proves her love for God. Instead, Rahner shows how a more intimate sense of unity between love for neighbor and God is found in scripture and tradition. He describes this relationship as being one of mutual conditioning.[39] At times, Rahner even suggests that love for neighbor is an antecedent condition for experiencing genuine love for God: "Love for God only comes to its own identity through its fulfillment in love for neighbor."[40] Throughout his work, he consistently affirms a mutuality between being transcendentally open to God's word and loving one's neighbor.[41]

Rahner's justification for proposing a unity between love for God and neighbor is both philosophical and theological. To examine this thesis adequately, we first need to explore why Rahner claims that our love for God must be mediated through intramundane communication, and then examine why this mediation necessarily involves love for one's neighbor. Rahner argues that divine–human communication is necessarily mediated due to the differences present in human finitude and God's incomprehensibility. Because God employs finite language and concepts to communicate divine love, it is inevitably the case that humanity's relationship to God is also necessarily mediated through the world.[42] Just as persons attain knowledge and self-presence through interactions with their environment, their love for God is also realized through their involvement in the world. Thus, humans express their love for God and their response to God's self-offer through their everyday actions. Furthermore, since God is the very ground of one's being and source of one's transcendence, the very idea of loving God in a direct, unmediated way risks objectifying God and reducing the divine to the limits of human categories:

> God is not an object towards which the intentionality of man can be directed in the same fragmentary way as it is towards the multiplicity of objects and persons encountered within the categories of intramundane experience.... God is always given as the subjectively and objectively all-becoming ground of experience.[43]

Human love for God, then, must be mediated, and it needs to be mediated in and through loving one's neighbor. Love of neighbor is not merely one among many moral acts but is "the one moral basic act in which man comes to himself and decides basically about himself."[44] Rahner offers several theological reasons to defend this thesis. First, he argues that the unity between love for God and neighbor resonates with scripture, especially the synoptic passage in which Christ says, "Whatever you have done to the least of my brothers and sisters, you have done it unto me" (Matthew 25:40). The unity of loves is also found in the Gospel of John, which characterizes God as present within each person. God cannot be loved and experienced in a "gnostic-mystic interiority alone." Instead, Rahner argues that, according to John, we love God present in each of us when we love our neighbor:

> The 'God in us' is really the one who alone can be loved and who is reached precisely in the love of our brother and in no other way, and that the love of neighbour encounters the love of God in *such* a way that it moves itself, and us with it, closer to the brother near by and attains both itself and the peak of perfection in the love of this brother, i.e., specifically as love of neighbour, and brings us to God by the love of our neighbour.[45]

Rahner also defends the unity between love for God and neighbor by arguing that a "yes" to God involves embracing God's will for us and striving to become the persons God created us to be. He claims that God creates us to be social beings who actualize ourselves by entering into the "mystery of love" with one another. Hence, self-realization is profoundly intersubjective; growing in our love for others is the only way we respond positively to God's self-communication and experience human fulfillment.

The Mystery of Human Freedom

It is important to note that, although Rahner affirms that our transcendental freedom to effect a fundamental option is actualized through our categorical choices, he does not view the relation between all categorical acts and one's fundamental option as a simple correlation. In other words, he rejects the prospect that one's ultimate "yes" or "no" to God is determined by the sum of one's moral and immoral deeds, each categorical action having equal value. He also dismisses the idea that one's last actions in life necessarily have the greatest weight in determining a fundamental option for God.[46] This is because we can never judge with certainty to what degree our individual acts are free. Just like any transcendental experience, it cannot be empirically isolated from other elements within our subjectivity and completely objectified. Consequently, freedom remains ambiguous, even though we continue to experience ourselves as free subjects. Rahner argues that, while our categorical acts determine who we become before God and ultimately our fundamental option, only those actions that are sufficiently "free" impact and shape our fundamental stance for and against God. He repeatedly acknowledges that human freedom is not pure or absolute: every categorical action consists of a mixture of freedom and imposed necessity. Since persons cannot completely objectify their freedom, they cannot with certainty judge the degree of freedom present in their actions:

> With regard to individual free actions in his life, the subject never has an absolute certainty about the subjective and therefore moral quality of these individual actions because, as real and as objectified in knowledge, these actions are always a synthesis of original freedom and imposed necessity, a synthesis which cannot be resolved completely in reflection.[47]

Thus, it is possible that an objectively wrong action may not transcendentally reflect a refusal of God's self-offer because it is not sufficiently free, while a seemingly decent person may in fact have rejected God's self-offer by choosing pride, egoism, and self-deception over a life dedicated to neighbor-love:

> In certain circumstances it is possible that nothing is hidden beneath an apparently very great offense because it can be just the phenomenon of a pre-personal situation, and behind the façade of bourgeois respectability there can be hidden a final, embittered and despairing "no" to God, and one that is really subjectively done and not just passively endured.[48]

Due to the mysterious character of human freedom on the categorical level, Rahner is thus arguing that persons cannot be absolutely confident about the moral status of each categorical action and its effect on their fundamental option. They cannot refer to a certain event in history and assert that at such a moment a radical "yes" or "no" to God took place.[49] As a result, he consistently emphasizes the need for epistemic humility when reflecting on one's own or another's fundamental option for or against God:

> The actual situation of a person's freedom . . . is not completely accessible to reflection, to an examination of conscience which would be understood as a definitive statement of absolute certainty. A person never knows with absolute certainty whether the objectively guilty character of his action, which he can perhaps establish unambiguously, is the objectification of a real and original decision of freedom saying "no" to God, or whether it is more in the nature of a manipulation which has been imposed upon him and which he endures, and which has about it the character of necessity.[50]

Overall, Rahner's claim that we cannot with certainty know our fundamental option from categorical moral acts is based on his belief in the mysterious nature of freedom as it is experienced in our concrete, existential situations.

In addition, out of a deep conviction that one's final self-disposal requires time, Rahner has further warrant to reject the idea of a simple correlation between specific categorical acts and one's transcendental stance toward God. He notes that each categorical action "receives its weight and proportion from the horizon of the whole of human existence."[51] Unlike the angels, presumably, persons are not able to dispose of themselves and effect a fundamental option in one temporal event; rather, due to human nature, persons need time to actualize their freedom and decide who they will become.[52] Rahner observes: "Since we ourselves are still coming to be in freedom, we do not exist with and behold this eternity, but in our passage through the multiplicity of the temporal we are performing this event of freedom, we are forming the eternity which we ourselves are and are becoming."[53] He argues that, although each human act of freedom strives toward a complete self-disposal, human nature resists allowing one free act to achieve a complete self-disposal and alter a person's entire being. Rahner refers to this resistance within human nature as "concupiscence."[54] Concupiscence anticipates one's free action and prevents it from fully transforming one's entire being. Rahner notes that concupiscence prevents a person from becoming completely absorbed in either good or evil in her lifetime. There is always a tension between nature (who one is) and who one wants to become; thus, there is always some potency remaining within a human being who is oriented toward further transcendence and becoming. Concupiscence ensures that persons never fully actualize their potentialities.

Of course, concupiscence does not preclude one from achieving a final self-disposal, a final orientation for or against God. Since it prevents persons from being completely good or evil during their lifetimes, concupiscence ensures that the possibility of altering one's fundamental option always exists during one's lifetime: "Freedom . . . is not finally and definitively actualized until it has actively passed through the deed of life and into the absolute powerlessness of death."[55] Persons who have grown in love for God and have been striving toward effecting a positive fundamental option may give in to the ever-present existential of sin and ultimately turn away from God. On the other hand, the existential of grace is always copresent, making possible the experience of conversion. A person who has increasingly refused God's self-offer may finally respond to grace and seek repentance. Rahner's hope for such a possibility is grounded in God's self-communication, which constantly calls each person to seek forgiveness and reunite with God in love. Rahner characterizes the moment of dying as representing the consummation of one's fundamental option: "With death comes the finality of man's basic option, which permeates his history and in which he disposes of himself in confrontation with God, set before him by world and history."[56]

Rahner acknowledges that the idea of persons deciding definitively against a loving relationship with God makes it hard to comprehend and accept that persons could be given this form of radical freedom. As difficult as it may be to grasp, however, he argues that the opposing view is absolutely nonsensical from the Christian point of view, for it denies that "freedom can really have something to do with God pure and simple."[57] It thus renders our life on earth and our process of becoming who we wish to be irrelevant to our destiny with God. In other words, if one accepts the contrasting view that persons cannot possibly offend against God, one must concede that there is no reason to take human freedom seriously; a person's history ceases to matter in an ultimate sense if it has no effect on one's relationship with God. Such a view, according to Rahner, is deeply antithetical to the core meaning of Christianity.

Threats to One's Freedom to Say "Yes" to God

If rejection of God's self-communication is simultaneously a rejection of authentic self-realization, why would anyone freely choose to reject God? Rahner responds that the possibility of sin as a permanent existential is present in our lives, making it possible for us to resist and turn away from the source of our being and fulfillment. He acknowledges how the power of other persons' sin pervasively affects every individual's sphere of freedom: "The situation of our own freedom bears the stamp of the guilt of others in a way which cannot be eradicated."[58] Our freedom to create who we finally want to be in our entirety is shaped and constrained by other persons' attitudes and actions in our culture and in history: "All of man's experience points in the direction that there are in fact objectifications of personal guilt in the world which, as the material for the free decisions of other persons, threaten these decisions, have a seductive effect upon them, and make free decisions painful."[59]

But to what extent, exactly, can the sin and guilt of persons and communities constrain an individual's freedom to respond positively to God's self-offer? Rahner's general position is that collective guilt impinges on, but does not destroy, our freedom to respond positively or negatively to God's self-communication.[60] He argues that, while our sphere of freedom can be greatly diminished or enhanced by others' freedom, our essential freedom is retained despite external and internal threats:

> By realizing my own freedom I also partly determine the sphere of freedom of others. True, I do not change their freedom, but the sphere in which their freedom is realized, hence this affects the possibilities of their subjective freedom. Freedom is always realized in the concrete sphere. Persons who realize their freedom are not the untouchable Monads envisaged by Leibnitz. Every free act of one person changes the objective possibilities of the free act of his neighbor, it enlarges, changes or limits the sphere of the other's freedom before this latter can freely intervene. Hence the realization of freedom is the concrete problem of human relations.[61]

At times, however, Rahner seems to recognize that our vulnerability to others runs deeper than merely changing the sphere of our freedom. In his analysis of power, Rahner speaks of a person's "innate possibility of acting spontaneously, without the previous consent of another, to interfere with and change the *actual constitution* of that other."[62] He argues that each person's power influences the eternal destiny of all persons affected by our actions:

> It is therefore clear that power acts in combination with this eternal freedom and contributes to the eternal result of the freedom of another. He is for ever not just such as he willed to be, but also such as

> became through me, the other. . . . What an enormous task is imposed on man, simply by the fact that he has power to act on the freedom of man![63]

In his article "The Dignity and Freedom of Man," Rahner describes external influences (material forces and other persons) as being capable of "seizing" persons who have yet to ratify their decision for or against God.[64] Consider the following ways he acknowledges the insidious effects of external threats to our freedom.

> There is no 'zone' of the person which is absolutely inaccessible to such influences from without. Every 'external' event can be significant and menacing for the ultimate salvation of the person, and is, therefore, subject to the law of the dignity of the person who as such can be degraded by some intervention from without.[65]

> Man, on account of uninvited influences exerted on him from without, is not simply and from the very start in lordly possession of complete control over his personal power of decision. He can be swept away involuntarily (before any action of his freedom takes place) to do actions which either lack freedom and responsibility completely or possess them only to a diminished degree, and which then become an obstacle to and restriction of the possibilities of his freedom for good. He can be corrupted in advance of his decision.[66]

Such descriptions of how a person's "actual constitution" can be changed by another's actions, of being "seized" by external influences, "swept away involuntarily" to commit unfree actions, "corrupted" before effecting a fundamental option, and so on, clearly demonstrate that Rahner does not view a person as autonomous from birth, always capable of exercising complete control over his will and actions by virtue of his reason. Such forms of corruption narrow the possibilities individuals have to choose good and ultimately say yes to God's self-communication. These external threats, in turn, give rise to internal threats, which tempt a person to turn away from God's call to love God and others and choose instead selfishness and egoism.

Recognizing that these external threats to one's capacity to say yes to God carry ethical implications, Rahner argues that persons have an obligation toward one another to ensure that all have a sphere in which to realize their freedom and become the persons God intends. He claims that the Church and secular society must, out of respect for each person's dignity, provide conditions that help persons realize their freedom.[67] In "The Dignity and Freedom of Man," he says, "Wherever (and in so far as) a certain freedom and security of the material conditions of life belong to the necessary practical prerequisite of personal freedom, they are sanctioned by the dignity of human freedom and must be demanded in the name of this freedom."[68] If certain material conditions are a prerequisite to freedom, it must be asked whether one's capacity for freedom to effect a fundamental option can be destroyed by a lack of these conditions or severe, interpersonal harm. If this is even conceivable for Rahner, then might the act of accepting God's self-communication actually be partly due to mere chance and fortune? In his best known writings on grace and freedom,[69] Rahner repeatedly renounces the possibility that one's response to God is contingent on luck: despite experiences of external threats, persons possessing reason are confronted with an inescapable responsibility for themselves:[70]

> One of the results of this situation of being threatened is that man inevitably finds himself either in a state of guilt or in a state of redemption, in so far as he has had any free control at all over himself. . . . As a spiritual person, control over himself is for him inescapable. If, however, he has control over himself, then he has control (implicitly or explicitly) over himself in accordance with all the existential dimensions of his being. He accepts, therefore, his concrete being (including the supernatural existential of this being), or he possesses it in the manner of rejection and then he is guilty.[71]

Although Rahner posits prerequisite conditions for freedom in "The Dignity and Freedom of Man," he nevertheless insists that individuals deprived of such conditions would still retain the capacity to say yes or no to God's self-communication:

> If, on the one hand, freedom considered simply in itself, i.e. freedom of exercise and not merely freedom in what is done, belongs to the absolute dignity of the person and if, on the other hand, it is dependent for its exercise in the concrete on conditions of an external and internal kind, then the concession of these possibilities of the exercise of freedom to a sufficiently large extent is demanded by the dignity of the person. To deprive the person totally of the scope for freedom would, therefore, still be a degradation of the person even when the thing to be done [effect a fundamental option][72] would still be capable without this concession of scope for freedom.[73]

Similarly, when considering difficult cases of individuals who appear to have had few options to say yes to God's offer of self-communication, Rahner is nevertheless adamant that they had sufficient opportunity. In the article "The Comfort of Time," he concludes:

> Apparently very little material is required for such total self-achievement. What we may sorrowfully be tempted to complain about as the poverty of opportunities for certain people (in the case of those who died young, etc.), will have to be regarded as the normal opportunity. . . . One must not overrate the significance of the difference in external situation for the proper achievement of man's existence. For otherwise it would be a strange arrangement of life by God, if in most cases of this free spiritual creature—which after all is called to realize its being freely—this realization did not come to its proper fulfillment.[74]

In this article, Rahner appeals to Christian hope as the ground of his belief that each person has sufficient capacity to realize freedom despite earthly contingencies. Two theological beliefs underlie this hope. First, God creates a human being for the purpose of being fully able to realize his or her true being by loving God and neighbor. Each human life is an answer to God's offer of self-communication. Second, Rahner claims that salvation necessarily includes both God's grace and a person's free act of accepting God's self-offer: "A salvation not achieved in freedom cannot be salvation."[75]

Conclusion

In his best known writings on grace and freedom, Rahner depicts the human person as confronted with the ever-present offer of God's self-communication, which represents "the innermost constitutive element of man" and promises a future of "fulfillment in the beatific vision, the direct knowledge of God face to face in love."[76] In every free act throughout their lives, persons are faced with the decision either to respond to God's self-communication by transcending themselves and surrendering in love to the incomprehensible God or turning away from the divine offer and remaining imprisoned within their own egoism. The freedom to accept God's self-communication is thus synonymous with becoming an authentic self who loves God and neighbor. As compelling and powerful as this narrative might be in offering a theological framework for individuals to assume freedom and responsibility for who they are becoming, it is questionable whether this theological anthropology is credible in the face of severe interpersonal harm. We must ask if it is indeed possible to defend any theology of freedom within the context of severe traumatization. To sharpen this question, we now turn to examine specifically the devastating impact of trauma on a person's sense of self, freedom, and relationality.

3

The Vulnerable Self and Loss of Agency

Trauma Theory and the Challenge to a Rahnerian Theology of Freedom and Grace

Having reviewed Rahner's theology of human freedom and God's grace, we are now ready to consider whether his theology of freedom resonates with and even illuminates the experience of persons whose lives have been shattered for some duration by severe acts of violence. In this chapter, I draw from vast research studies to examine the effects of one particular trauma—prolonged incestuous abuse. After offering reasons for focusing on this particular group of trauma survivors, I explore the prevalence of both intrafamilial and extra-familial sexual abuse, and analyze how the effects of incestuous abuse impact victims' sense of self, their exercise of autonomy, and their capacity for relationality.[1] This is important because, if Rahner's theological anthropology hopes to endure as a credible account of the relation between the human self, freedom, and God's grace, it needs to account for populations of trauma victims such as those incestuously abused as children.

Rationale for Selecting Incest Survivors as Trauma Test Cases

While an examination of any population of traumatized persons would be appropriate for the purpose of exploring the central questions of this book, I choose to focus on female incest victim-survivors as a case study for three main reasons.[2] First, research on trauma victims has revealed that the degree to which an event will overwhelm and traumatize a person generally increases the younger a victim is; one's sense of self and the strength of one's psychological defenses clearly develop through time.[3] For this reason, the effects of interpersonal harm on sexually abused children serve as a clear "worst case scenario" for how pervasively one's sense of self, relationality, and agency can be damaged. Second, a majority of research studies on various forms of trauma suggests that, for several reasons, victims of human-induced trauma (as opposed to traumas related to natural disasters) generally experience greater degrees of traumatization. Most significantly, this is due to the fact that victims of human-induced traumas experience firsthand the horrific degree of cruelty that persons are capable of inflicting on one another; thus, they suffer from intensified forms of shattered trust and betrayal. The experience of child sexual abuse by a relative represents one of the most severe forms of betrayal and shattered trust, and it once again serves as a worst case scenario for how interpersonal violence affects persons' freedom and relationality. Third, the prevalence of incestuous abuse in the United States and throughout the world guards against the temptation to bracket this population of traumatized persons as an extreme and rare exception to the "normal" person whose ultimate freedom is not completely vulnerable to interpersonal harm. Given the prevalence of child sexual abuse overall and incestuous abuse in particular, it is statistically likely that this population of trauma victims forms a significant percentage of members in religion-based communities. Since this would be true, therefore, of Christian communities as well as others, the presence of trauma victims raises sharply the question of the ongoing viability of a Christian theology of freedom such as Karl Rahner's. It also raises a number of ethical and theological implications for such communities, which I will address in chapter 6.

Prevalence of Incestuous Abuse

Given the predominance of the psychoanalytic tradition's claim that the etiology of psychological disorders lies in intrapsychic conflicts rather than externally caused traumas, the reality of childhood incestuous abuse was seriously minimized in our culture until the 1970s. Prior to this time, very little research on child sexual abuse had been conducted.[4] It was only during the 1970s, when feminist scholars and incest survivors began to speak out publicly against domestic violence and child sexual abuse, that silence about the prevalence of incestuous abuse and severity of its traumatic effects was broken.

In 1983, Diana Russell published the first study on the prevalence of extrafamilial and intrafamilial child sexual abuse and incest victims in a nonclinical population.[5] Interviewing a random sample of 930 women who lived in San Francisco, she found the prevalence rate for child sexual abuse to be 38 percent. As for incestuous abuse, 16 percent of the women reported sexual abuse by some relative, and 4.5 percent reported incestuous abuse with their fathers.[6] Incestuous abuse was defined as "any kind of exploitative sexual conduct or attempted contact that occurred between relatives, no matter how distant the relationship, before the victim turned eighteen years old."[7]

In her analysis of the data, Russell claims that the 16 percent prevalence rate is most likely lower than the actual percentage of incest victims in the United States, since the populations where the highest rates of incest occur were not included; such populations include the homeless, those in psychiatric hospitals, prisons, brothels, residential alcohol and other drug rehabilitation programs, and battered women's shelters. In addition, due to dissociative amnesia, many women genuinely may not be in a position to recall incestuous abuse. Finally, due to the shame and stigma attached to being sexually abused, it is also likely that some of the women who were interviewed may have chosen not to reveal their experiences to the interviewer.[8]

Since this study, there has been another research study, conducted by the *Los Angeles Times* in 1986, that focused on the national prevalence of child sexual abuse and incestuous abuse. Interviews with a group of 1,481 female subjects showed a 27 percent prevalence rate of child sexual abuse and 8 percent prevalence for incest.[9] As with the 1983 study, it is very likely that these rates are much lower than the actual prevalence of sexual abuse; in this case, there are at least three main reasons: the interviews were conducted by telephone; each interview lasted only thirty minutes; and each person was asked only four questions about child sexual abuse.[10]

It is beyond the limits of this chapter to analyze in greater depth the prevalence rates in these and other studies. The relevant point to keep in mind here is that the rates obtained for child sexual abuse and incest in both studies are significant and alarming; it is no longer an option to view child sexual abuse and incest as an aberrant sexual practice. In 1990, the U.S. Advisory Board on Child Abuse and Neglect referred to child abuse as a "national emergency" and recommended "replacement of the existing child protection system."[11] The results from these studies call for urgent attention to both intra- and extrafamilial child sexual abuse, immediate intervention for abused children, and new programs for prevention.

To gain clarity on the central question posed in this book—namely, the challenge trauma raises to Christian theologies of freedom—we turn now to the effects of child sexual abuse, particularly incest. Describing the effects of such abuse, which seem to take on a life of their own, is necessary to show the pervasive damage of incest to one's self, freedom, and capacity for healthy relationships with God and others.

Traumatizing Effects of Incestuous Abuse

For both children and adults in general, the primary form of protection against being physically and psychologically overwhelmed and traumatized is secure relationships with others: "As long as people are able to imagine some way of staving off the inevitable, or as long as they feel taken care of by someone stronger than themselves, psychological and biological systems seem to be protected against becoming overwhelmed."[12] Due to their immature stages of development, infants and children need a great degree of consistent external protection, nurture, and support to comfort and soothe them; only through interacting with trusted caretakers do they learn how to regulate their internal states and responses to external stressors.

Besides the fact that relatedness to others helps children master self-regulation, interactions with others are crucial for the formation and development of one's sense of self. According to major psychological theories such as developmental psychology, attachment theory, and object relations theory, the self forms and develops within a constant dialectic of relating to others (attachment) and exploring and engaging the world (self-mastery and autonomy). Experiencing a sense of safety and protection by her primary caretakers enables a child to feel sufficiently secure to venture away for a time and explore her emerging sense of self and the world. As the psychiatrist Judith Herman notes, during stages of normal childhood development, a child's emergent sense of self and autonomy is dependent on inner representations of trustworthy and dependable caretakers; when children feel threatened, they can psychologically return to these inner representations of safety in order to feel soothed and regulate their emotions.[13] When parents affirm children in their basic processes of development, children feel valued, affirmed, and respected, and this motivates them to master more skills and further explore their environment with curiosity. Learning how to accomplish these basic developmental tasks increases children's self-esteem and sense of competence. Throughout this process, children develop autonomy—"a sense of their own separateness within a relationship."[14] This dynamic of first venturing away from one's caretaker and further developing a sense of self and autonomy and then returning to one's protector to gain security and affirmation continues in differing degrees from infancy through adolescence.

What happens to a child's developing sense of self and capacity for autonomy if one of her care providers not only fails to protect her from external threats but also inflicts injury and violates her bodily and psychic integrity? At the most basic level, sexual abuse threatens the security and attachment to one's care provider—one of the key necessary ingredients for survival itself and development of a sense of self during childhood. Herman describes the impact of abuse on children in the following way.

> Repeated trauma in childhood forms and deforms the personality. The child trapped in an abusive environment is faced with formidable tasks of adaptation. She must find a way to preserve a sense of trust in people who are untrustworthy, safety in a situation that is unsafe, control in a situation that is terrifyingly unpredictable, power in a situation of helplessness . . . with the only means at her disposal, an immature system of psychological defenses.[15]

Many therapists who work with abused children attest to children's primary need to believe their parents are loving, benevolent, and just. These beliefs stem from their basic need to seek love, preserve trust, and remain attached to their parents even if the latter are perpetrators of horrific abuse: "To preserve her faith in her parents, [a child] must reject the first and most obvious conclusion that something is terribly wrong with them. She will go to any lengths to construct an explanation for her fate that absolves her parents of all blame and responsibility."[16] One of the most effective defense mechanisms used to deny the reality of chronic overwhelming violence for both children and adults involves dissociating (commonly described as "splitting off") violent, traumatic events from one's consciousness. Dissociation refers to the capacity to separate the elements of the traumatic experience—emotions, thoughts, sensation, location, time, and meaning—into shattered fragments that defy conscious integration.

Dissociating occurs in varying degrees: persons may experience a sense of unreality, feel completely disconnected from their bodies, or experience complete dissociative amnesia of the event and retain no conscious memory of the abuse. Dissociative amnesia frequently lasts for many months or years, or it may persist throughout a lifetime. In the most extreme conditions of early, prolonged child abuse, some children dissociate to such an extent that the memories of the abuse that are "split off" form separate personality fragments. These fragments, referred to as "alters" (formerly called multiple personalities), have their own names and contain certain memories of the abuse.[17] For

Herman, the alters "make it possible for the child victim to cope resourcefully with the abuse while keeping both the abuse and her coping strategies outside of ordinary awareness."[18]

For most children who are sexually abused for a prolonged period, dissociation as a sole coping mechanism is often not effective in consistently denying the reality of the abuse.[19] When dissociation fails, children, like all victims of trauma, seek to make some sense of why they have been chosen to be victims of abuse. Since children cannot bear to face the reality that their parents are doing unjustifiably cruel things to them, the only option they have left is to take full responsibility themselves for the abuse and conclude that there is something intrinsically bad about them that leads their parents (in most cases, their fathers) to act sexually toward them. Blaming herself and taking responsibility also gives a child an illusory sense of control over the abuse and the hope that it can end if she changes from being bad to good. Sadly, in the case of prolonged sexual abuse, nothing the child does ends the abuse; this only reinforces her negative feelings about herself and her own inability to prevent the abuse. Even sexually abused children who have fully dissociated the abuse and retain no conscious memories feel a profound innate badness at the core of their self-understanding.

Since dissociation, amnesia, and self-blame actually enable the sexually abused child to remain attached to her parents, one of the obvious consequences is that the abuse is not revealed, exposed, or stopped. As a result, the child becomes isolated from any external social support that might help restore a sense of safety and protection, and she often becomes subject to further chronic abuse. Due to chronic abuse and the secrecy and isolation it produces, most children experience a host of posttraumatic stress symptoms. These can be categorized into at least three behavioral patterns: (1) a reexperiencing of the traumatic event, which results in persistent forms of hyperarousal; (2) response to hyperarousal, which includes forms of emotional numbing such as avoidance, dissociation, and/or inducing autonomic arousal; and (3) behavioral tendencies to reenact the past trauma compulsively.

Persistent Forms of Hyperarousal

Since incestuous abuse overwhelms children's capacity for self-protection, many children experience persistent intrusions of traumatic memory, which commonly take the form of intrusive flashbacks and nightmares. Reexperiencing the traumatic event, however, does not necessarily mean cognitively remembering the actual events. When victims of incestuous abuse experience total or partial psychogenic amnesia, they reexperience the trauma in other forms, for example, intense bodily or emotional sensations, terrifying sensory perceptions, obsessional preoccupations, and behavioral reenactments of past trauma.[20] The psychologist Lenore Terr repeatedly found, for instance, that sexually abused children who could not verbally recall memories of the abuse still reenacted the past trauma during their playing and other forms of behavior. "Posttraumatic play . . . is a grim, long-lasting and particularly contagious form of childhood repetitive behavior."[21]

Such intrusive reenactments of the trauma cause chronic physiological and psychological states of hyperarousal, disrupting the body's regulation of arousal and stress adaptation.[22] Autonomic arousal by itself is an essential adaptive instinct in response to threats to survival: one's central nervous system becomes activated, resulting in an adrenalin rush that helps to assess the danger quickly and accurately, enabling survival through "fight or flight." During a traumatic event, however, a person's ability to defend herself is overwhelmed and ineffective; as a result, her self-defense system becomes disorganized and confused, and she begins to experience a persistent state of hyperarousal. One of the most common symptoms is constant hypervigilance in which one's acoustic startle response (ASR) reacts to the slightest environmental stimuli as if everything in one's environment represented potential danger. Other common forms of hyperarousal include irritability, angry outbursts, restlessness, difficulty concentrating, and difficulty sleeping.

Unfortunately, experiencing persistent states of hyperarousal becomes even more entrenched and maladaptive when the traumatic stressor is not one isolated event but is repeated and chronic.[23] In regard to children who are being repeatedly abused, hyperarousal disturbs every aspect of their development and overall functioning ability. At the most basic level, an abused child's normal biological cycles of sleeping, waking, and eating are usually chronically disrupted. Attention deficit disorder, sleep disorders, eating disorders, gastrointestinal problems, and other bodily distress symptoms are common long-term effects of hyperarousal for incestuously abused children.[24]

Such persistent physiological and psychological states of arousal can cause permanent changes on cognitive, affective, and neurobiological levels. Incest victims' cognitive ability to process information about their external environment and their internal states is altered in several ways.[25] Many incest victims have problems being attentive to their environment, which obviously impedes their ability to assess potential danger accurately. Furthermore, since children's ASR becomes activated at the slightest noise and they perceive innocuous stimuli as threats that spark physiological arousal, they have a lower threshold for tolerating mild to moderate stressors. As a result, children respond by feeling intensely and chronically confused, agitated, empty, isolated, anxious, panicked, furious, and despairing, and they have profound difficulty regulating their emotions in order to experience emotional comfort and calm.[26]

Constriction via Emotional Numbing, Dissociation, and Autonomic Arousal

As an attempt to counteract these persistent forms of hyperarousal, incest victims (and others suffering from PTSD) seek to avoid trauma-related emotions in a variety of ways. The most common responses are emotional numbing, dissociation, and/or inducing autonomic arousal. Frequently, the most common way of responding to chronic hyperarousal for traumatized persons is to experience a sense of withdrawal and detachment from emotions and physical sensations.[27] When emotional numbing does not occur "naturally," many traumatized persons abuse alcohol and drugs as a way to attain emotional numbness and escape unbearable symptoms of hyperarousal.[28] For incestuously abused children, emotional numbing may also involve dissociative states that occur at behavioral, affect, sensation, and knowledge levels.[29] Besides dissociating during sexual abuse as already described, abused children tend to grow increasingly dependent on this defense mechanism to escape negative emotions and "split them off" from consciousness.

While dissociation can function as a defense mechanism to provide a protective sense of detachment from reality, it does not always achieve emotional numbness. There are times when dissociation is still accompanied by extreme negative emotions. When this occurs, many incest victims experience a form of dissociation that leads to a compulsion to attack the body. The only way that abused children can break through this sense of "annihilation" and dysphoria is by experiencing some kind of jolt to the body, and they resort to some form of extreme autonomic arousal such as self-mutilation: "The initial injuries often produce no pain at all. The mutilation continues until it produces a powerful feeling of calm and relief; physical pain is much preferable to the emotional pain that it replaces. As one survivor explains: 'I do it to prove I exist.'"[30] Other forms of self-destructive extreme autonomic arousal that commonly serve to regulate incest victims' internal emotional states include fasting, purging or vomiting, compulsive sexual behavior, compulsive risk taking or exposure to danger, and drug use.

Compulsive Tendencies to Reenact Trauma

It is a common behavioral pattern for traumatized persons to seek compulsively to reexpose themselves to situations similar to their particular form of trauma.

Most forms of repetition of the traumatic event cause further harm for the victims and those persons related to them, and often become life-threatening. There are many complex reasons for reenacting past trauma. Some therapists theorize that this behavior is an attempt to gain control over the past traumatic event. Certain incest victims do express a conscious desire to resolve past trauma when they find themselves in threatening situations. However, most are not consciously aware that they are compulsively reenacting the trauma, and they experience a feeling of involuntariness when engaging in these repetitious acts.[31]

Compulsively reenacting the trauma generally takes one of three forms: acts of self-destructiveness, harm to others, and revictimization. There is a consistent pattern in many research studies demonstrating a link between child sexual abuse and self-destructive acts.[32] The earlier the abuse occurs during childhood, the more likely the child is to engage in self-destruction in order to regulate her negative emotions. A high percentage also commonly attempt suicide, an action that stems from their desperate desire to seek an end to their self-hatred, despair, and of course life itself.[33]

Another form of reenacting the trauma is harming others. Some incestuously abused children painfully recount memories of sexually abusing other children or encouraging them to perform sexual acts for the perpetrator—acts that reinforce the victims' self-hatred.[34] Typically, however, this population consists mostly of boys; sexually abused girls are statistically less likely to direct their aggression on others, and usually engage in the aforementioned self-destructive actions.[35]

Finally, traumatized victims of incestuous abuse are especially vulnerable to revictimization. In Diana Russell's study, whereas 48 percent of women who had no incest histories reported sexual assault at some point in their lives, 82 percent of incest victims reported subsequent sexual assault.[36] Numerous studies have found that victims of child sexual abuse are at high risk for becoming prostitutes, and victims of father-daughter incest are four times more likely to agree to pose for pornography.[37] One factor contributing to these high risks is that a significant percentage of sexually abused girls run away from home, only to be sexually abused on the streets. When seeking to explain the dynamics of revictimization, Herman is careful to correct the notion that abused women are masochistic and actively seek out revictimization; instead, repeated abuse "is passively experienced as a dreaded but unavoidable fate."[38] Another factor contributing to sexual revictimization involves the effects of the abuse on a child's sexuality. Barbara Krahé notes that some incest victims are prone to revictimization due to the negative effects of the abuse on their developing sexuality. A significant number of sexually abused girls sexualize their behavior toward males. Numerous studies have found that such sexualized behavior includes sexual preoccupation, seductive behavior, excessive masturbation, sex play with others, genital exposure, and the sexual victimization of others.[39] During adolescence, sexual abuse victims tend to be sexually active earlier and engage in sexual activities with more partners than nonabused female adolescents—activities that statistically lead to higher rates of victimization.

Effects of Incestuous Abuse on Self-Concept

While many of these posttraumatic stress symptoms function as defense mechanisms to enable the sexually abused child to survive, chronic use of them results in a severely fragmented self. Herman describes this fragmentation in the following way.

> All the structures of the self—the image of the body, the internalized images of others, and the values and ideals that lend a sense of coherence and purpose—are invaded and systematically broken down. . . . Whereas the victim of a single acute trauma may say she is "not herself" since the event, the victim of chronic trauma may lose the sense that she has a self.[40]

Before examining in depth the impact of sexual abuse overall on children's sense of self, it is necessary to clarify the concept of self that is employed in the psychological literature. While there is no definition of self that is universally accepted in the social sciences, many psychologists who study the impact of trauma on persons find it helpful to distinguish two aspects of the self that are experientially interrelated and are commonly referred to as the I-self and the me-self.[41] The I-self is defined as the subjective self that actively initiates, organizes, chooses, and interprets experience. The primary aspects of the I-self commonly include (1) self-awareness: being aware of one's internal states, needs, thoughts, and emotions; (2) self-coherency: a stable sense of a unified entity distinct from other selves; (3) self-continuity: the sense that, despite changes, one remains the same, underlying self over time; and (4) self-agency: the sense that one has control over one's actions, thoughts, and emotions.[42] The me-self, by contrast, is often referred to as the objective self that is evaluated and determined by the I-self; in other words, the me-self is reflected in one's self-concept.[43] It is pervasively shaped by one's perceptions of interactions and relations with other persons and the world.[44]

The impact of child sexual abuse on self-agency is central to my subsequent evaluations of Karl Rahner's theology of freedom. I will defer consideration of self-agency, however, in order first to examine the impact of child sexual abuse on the other aspects of self-concepts. These are not finally unrelated to agency.

As for self-awareness, persistent states of hyperarousal greatly vitiate a child's capacity to learn how to identify and be conscious of her needs, thoughts, and emotions. Why is this the case? Hypervigilance, which diverts their focus and energy from learning how to identify and express their own needs, thoughts, and desires, causes children to focus on potential external threats. It is widely observed that abused children become very attuned—often unconsciously—to the internal states of their abusive parents rather than their own. This allows them to anticipate and meet the perpetrator's needs in the hope that one can pacify and please him, thus attempting to avoid further physical, sexual, and/or psychological abuse.[45] In other words, the developmental tasks of becoming in touch with one's needs and asserting a growing sense of autonomy are sacrificed for the good of survival and warding off further abuse.

Moreover, children's responses to hyperarousal—various forms of emotional numbing—further interfere with their capacity to be cognizant of their own needs and emotions. As a way to counteract intense, negative emotions of hyperarousal, many sexually abused children and adolescents lose the ability to decipher messages from their autonomic nervous system to interpret and articulate to themselves and others how they are feeling.[46] Of course, if they are abused as very young children, they never learn how to develop this ability adequately in the first place. Seeking desperately to avoid extreme emotions, they avoid introspection in the attempt to ward off any form of awareness about past events. Research findings have consistently shown that abused children report fewer descriptions of feelings and introspection than nonabused children.[47]

Self-coherency, the second aspect of the I-self, is commonly defined as "having a sense of being a non-fragmented, physical whole with boundaries."[48] Self-coherency implies a minimal sense of wholeness and integrity within one's identity. Sexual abuse undermines coherency on multiple levels. Having one's bodily boundaries repeatedly violated impedes one from developing a sense of space that is respected between oneself and others. Similarly, the therapist Jon Allen observes that sexual abuse leads to severe internal conflicts within children that obstruct the formation of an integrated sense of self.[49] How is a child to reconcile, for instance, a "good day-time daddy" with a nighttime monster who sexually terrifies and violates her? Such disparate, usually horrific, traumatic experiences defy integration and are thus dissociated and "split off" from consciousness. Depersonalization, the sense of one's mind being separated from the body, also undermines a unified sense of self. Dissociation can become so severe that it leads to a sense of "complete disconnection from others and disintegration of the self."[50] Incest victim-survivors with dissociative identity disorder who experience different "alters" that may conflict with one another exemplify the most extreme form of lacking self-coherency. Dissociation thus interferes with the normal process that occurs in later adolescence of integrating various personality characteristics.

A third aspect of the I-self—self-continuity—involves perceiving one's identity as relatively stable across time. The psychiatrist Daniel Stern refers to it as "having the sense of enduring, of a continuity with one's own past so that one 'goes on being' and can even change while remaining the same."[51] Remembering one's past is obviously integral in developing a narrative of who one has become. Experiencing large memory gaps from different time periods that result from severe dissociation and amnesia clearly undermines one's identity. Again, persons with dissociative identity disorder exemplify most clearly how sexual abuse can give rise to a discontinuous sense of self.

As for the impact of sexual abuse on the child's me-self, the most pervasive effects are profound negative self-esteem and self-hatred.[52] Unlike nonabused children, who overwhelmingly express a positive bias toward themselves, sexually abused children consistently report themselves in a very negative light, feeling a profound sense of innate badness.[53] The reasons for such a negative self-concept are various. To begin, the very experience of sexual violation involves being objectified and used for the satisfaction of another. Experiencing one's own desires and needs as being utterly disregarded gives rise to intense degrees of lack of self-worth and dignity. The fact that the violation is sexual adds another stigmatized dimension of feeling defiled, dirty, and damaged. If a child or an adolescent experiences any form of emotional or sexual gratification from the abuse, she feels an additional burden of guilt and shamefulness, which further reinforces her sense of inherent badness.

In addition, "failing" to protect oneself from bodily violation and simultaneously feeling threatened, helpless, and out of control causes profound feelings of rage, humiliation, and shame directed at the me-self. Since it would be too dangerous to express this anger and fear toward the perpetrator, children usually turn this anger in on themselves and blame themselves for the abuse. Furthermore, being vulnerable to revictimization contributes to a sense of inefficacy, incompetence, and inadequacy, frequently trapping the victim in a persistent condition of learned helplessness.

As if the aforementioned assaults were not enough to damage pervasively one's me-self, it is unfortunately very common for sexual perpetrators to reinforce all of these negative self-beliefs. Often, sexual perpetrators are cruel and sadistic, and they have an uncanny ability to detect and exploit their victims' psychological vulnerabilities. Many perpetrators frequently inflict verbal abuse on their victims, degrading, insulting, and blaming them for the sexual abuse. Children internalize these opinions from their abusers, and this further perpetuates and strengthens their perceived inherent badness.

To say that sexual abuse causes negative self-esteem, although accurate, fails miserably to convey adequately the extent of damage to one's self-concept. In her work with female adults and adolescents who were sexually abused as children, Herman notes how victims' self-hatred is so severe that they often report feeling nonhuman, as though they are "witches, vampires, whores, dogs, rats or snakes."[54] One incest victim-survivor describes her core self in the following way: "I am filled with black slime. If I open my mouth, it will pour out. I think of myself as the sewer silt that a snake would breed upon."[55]

How do sexually abused girls and adolescents cope with perceiving their core selves as innately bad and evil? Desperately desiring to be normal, the majority of incest victims seek to hide their "true" self that feels defiled, unworthy, and despairing, and project a "false" good self to gain approval from their social world. Although some sexually abused girls begin to "act out" with aggression and delinquency, most sexual abuse victims successfully conceal many of their dysfunctional psychological behaviors. In Cameron's study, many adult incest victims described adolescence as a time when they were silently obsessed with desiring to die while outwardly attempting to act well-adjusted.[56]

While the defense mechanisms of sexually abused children and adolescents make it possible for many to exude convincingly a false "normal" self and survive, the inevitable cost is utter fragmentation of the self. They cannot integrate knowledge of themselves and their reality, their memories of the abuse, their emotions, and their bodily experiences into a coherent whole. As incest victims mature and become adults, these defense mechanisms become increasingly inadequate for handling their daily tasks and demands. Some incest victim-survivors who manage to appear well-adjusted through their twenties or thirties only then begin to experience an intolerable degree of posttraumatic stress symptoms.[57] Specifically, they experience severe posttraumatic stress symptoms, endure episodes of severe depression and anxiety, and express fear that they are going insane or will die. For many survivors, it is only at this time that the damaging effects of past sexual abuse on their autonomy and capacity for life-giving relationships become fully evident. In the following two sections focusing on autonomy and relationality, it will become clear that the negative impact of child sexual abuse on the I-self and the me-self also impedes developing a healthy sense of self-agency and capacity for cultivating healthy relationships.

Effects of Incestuous Abuse on Autonomy

There is much debate in philosophy about which accounts of agency and autonomy are most defensible in light of our contemporary appreciation for the pervasive influences of socialization on one's sense of self and agency. For the purpose of this book, I ask the reader to bracket this debate and accept a general, broad definition of autonomy/agency as a sense of control over one's actions, thoughts, and emotions,[58] and the ability to deliberate (in a rational, affective manner) and freely choose actions that cohere with one's life plan.[59] One's life plan consists of values, beliefs, goals, and ideals that make life meaningful and fulfilling. To put it most simply, a person who is autonomous has a general sense of being in control of her life and knows who she aspires to become. She is able to ask and answer the question: "What do I really want, need, care about, value, etc.?"[60] This is, of course, not the full-blown sense of freedom proposed by Rahner, but it is sufficient here as we try to understand the most obvious impact of child sexual abuse on capacities for self-determination.

A broad consensus exists among therapists who work with traumatized incest victims that these victims' capacity to realize their agency and autonomy has been severely harmed by the effects of prolonged, incestuous abuse. Herman argues: "For those who aspire to an image of free womanhood, incest is as destructive for women as genital mutilation or the binding of feet."[61] Incest diminishes the development of at least three capacities considered necessary for autonomy—capacities to (1) establish physical and psychological boundaries that form a distinct sense of self; (2) construct a basic life plan that includes a sense of what gives one meaning, fulfillment, and a vision of the kind of person one is striving to become; and (3) reflect on one's options and choose actions that are coherent with one's sense of self and life plan.

Developing a distinct sense of self with personal boundaries is a necessary precondition for the latter two capacities required for autonomy. As social scientific research demonstrates, having one's bodily integrity repeatedly violated obstructs the ability to develop a sufficient sense of boundaries (physical, social, and behavioral) with respect to oneself and others. When one is being sexually abused, only the perpetrator's needs matter; the incest victim's own will, needs, desires, and values are obviously disregarded and viewed as insignificant. This experience of being physically overpowered, trapped, and sexually violated derails a child's developmental tasks of self-differentiation—distinguishing one's own needs, desires, and goals from others'. One incest survivor expressed, for example, the sense that she didn't know "where she began and ended."[62] Many adult incest survivors continue to struggle with the inability to view themselves as distinct from others. This lack of a clear sense of where one's bodily boundaries end and another person's boundaries begin also impedes one's development of psychological boundaries: "Many survivors have such profound deficiencies in self-protection that they can barely imagine themselves in a position of agency or choice. The idea of saying no to the emotional demands of a parent, spouse, lover, or authority figure may be practically inconceivable."[63] Rather than pursuing the adult task of self-differentiation (discerning one's desires, goals, and life priorities), they often become one-sidedly consumed with caring for the needs of others, whether this takes the form of working in a service profession or attempting to meet the needs of abusive male partners.

Constructing a life plan and discerning what matters most to an individual is the second developmental task of agency—a capacity that is severely impeded by incestuous abuse. Constructing a life plan involves being self-reflective and self-aware, possessing at least a minimal sense of self-worth, and being able to imagine a future for oneself. As mentioned above, self-awareness is commonly lacking to a significant extent in adult incest victims, making it difficult to identify their needs, internal states, priorities, and goals. In their daily quest merely to survive, many incest victims evade self-reflection as a means to avoid traumatic memories and their subsequent negative emotions. Often, they repress past abuse for decades or for a lifetime and do not understand how their past is influencing their present self-concept or behavior. For instance, Russell found in her study that none of the incest victims consciously saw connections between their incestuous abuse and other forms of revictimization (rape, prostitution, domestic violence, their addiction to drugs and alcohol, etc.).[64]

Furthermore, to be motivated to think about and construct a life plan, one needs at least a minimal sense of self-worth to make the basic assumption that one's values and goals matter. Unfortunately, given past abusive experiences that have told them otherwise, many incest victims have trouble believing that they do matter. As we have seen, low self-esteem and self-hatred further undermine self-worth. In many research studies, incest victims have such deformed self-worth that they often express the sense that they do not deserve the "normal" rewards of family, love, fulfilling employment, and financial success.[65]

Being able to imagine a future with constructive possibilities is also necessary insofar as it offers persons the hope and motivation to reflect on their goals and dreams. This imaginative possibility is impeded by the long-term effects of incestuous abuse. As Leslie Berger notes, many incest victims are consumed by posttraumatic stress symptoms like intrusive memories, dissociative episodes, nightmares, and sadness: "Their abuse histories tended to occupy so much emotional space and take up so much energy that thoughts about the future were all but obliterated."[66] Furthermore, incest victims' ability to form dreams and goals about the future is undermined by their profoundly negative worldview.[67] The social psychologist Ronnie Janoff-Bulman observes that one of the most pervasive long-term effects of incest is a belief that the world is cruel and unfair and does not provide sufficient safety; when they do think about the future, incest victims are often preoccupied with fear about the harm that may befall them.[68] Berger also discovered that fears of being unsafe and revictimized influenced many incest victims' belief that they had very few (if any) options in life.[69]

Even if an incest victim is able to master the aforementioned tasks of establishing a sense of boundaries and constructing a life plan, many of the physical, psychological, and behavioral effects of incest hinder her from the third task of actively pursuing and realizing her goals. Many incest victims struggle with the ability to reflect on their immediate options and choose actions coherent with their life plans. To accomplish this consistently, a person must be able to comprehend the relevant facts and circumstances of her situation to choose actions that best cohere with her life plan. As noted, cognitive and affective skills of incest victims are often stunted and deformed by the abuse and subsequent PTSD symptoms. These diminished cognitive and affective abilities impede their ability to assess what is currently happening to them. Consequently, incest victims commonly have difficulty accurately assessing their situations and often doubt the accuracy of their perceptions. This inhibits their capacity to reflect on appropriate options and choose the best action to protect them from the threat of external stimuli. Traumatized persons, including women who suffered from childhood sexual abuse, often exhibit a fight-or-flight reaction, acting impulsively rather than being able to discern their emotional states and reflect cognitively on possible options. Besides feeling ashamed of their lack of control over responses, they exhibit an impulsivity that inevitably makes it difficult for them to protect themselves in threatening situations and to choose the best option for promoting their flourishing.

In addition, being repeatedly sexually violated engenders a profound sense of loss of control and inefficacy, which hinders an incest survivor's motivation and ability to initiate actions that are coherent with her life plan. Sexually abused girls not paralyzed by fear who attempt to resist their perpetrators are often punished psychologically and/or physically until they become passive and docile. The unpredictable nature of chronic sexual abuse further increases an abused child's or adolescent's sense of lacking any control over her body and life. Being repeatedly unable to protect oneself leads to an entrenched form of "learned helplessness," a belief that one is incapable of effectively changing one's life. As a result, feeling chronically powerless often persists throughout incest victims' lives, which exacerbates their sense of feeling out of control. Many incest victim-survivors react to daily stressors in adulthood by involuntarily dissociating. Some adult incest survivors report completely "spacing out" when confronted with a stressor such as a conflict with a boss. Experiencing such a loss of control obviously impedes incest survivors' ability to manage stressful situations effectively and ultimately break out of the repetitive cycle of disempowerment to realize their goals.

Furthermore, the issue of low self-esteem again appears, since it undermines survivors' motivation to pursue and accomplish their goals consistently. Berger notes that some incest victims feel acute anxiety when they are successful at work and often resort to self-defeating behaviors to jeopardize their success.[70] In her study, they tended to report feeling "safer" by keeping a lower profile at work. Victims in this scenario are consequently less likely to be productive and succeed, which reinforces their feelings of inefficacy; the downward spiral of negative self-esteem continues, impeding their ability to realize who they wish to become.

Lastly, permanent physiological and neurobiological changes resulting from child sexual abuse cause increased risk for many serious somatic and mental illnesses. They thereby also impede a person from actualizing her plans and dreams. Common somatic illnesses include chronic sleep disorders, digestive disorders, obesity, gynecological problems, chronic pain, and neurological problems. Common mental illnesses include dissociative identity disorder, borderline personality disorder, major anxiety, and depressive episodes. These psychiatric illnesses often lead to chronic suicidality, which frequently results in attempted suicides as well as actual deaths.[71]

Overall, the effects of past incestuous abuse conspire to thwart incest survivors' development of capacities for acting autonomously on a daily basis and for achieving a basic sense of self-determination. Just as incestuous abuse affects one's ability to cultivate a positive relationship with one's self and realize goals, it frequently disrupts the formation of positive relationships with others and God, a subject to which we now turn.

Effects of Incestuous Abuse on Relationships with Others and God

As incestuously abused females enter adulthood, their fragmented selves negatively impinge on their ability to form healthy, stable, intimate relationships with other persons. Due to the betrayal of trust in their families of origin and their negative self-esteem, adult incest victims are desperate to find care, protection, and external validation of themselves. Simultaneously, they are deeply afraid of trusting anyone and fear being abandoned or abused. These conflicting desires make it very difficult to establish and enjoy authentic, intimate friendships and sexual relationships. Most often, their abusive families have isolated them from others, thwarting their process of developing social skills needed for connection; being silent about the abuse for so many years also prevents them from experiencing what it is like to share one's intimate thoughts and feelings with friends or family members. Furthermore, incest victims' negative self-esteem impedes their ability to form friendships and to believe that they have positive things to offer others.

In response to their past abusive relationships, incest victims' attitudes toward relationships vary. Some survivors feel threatened by the prospect of intimacy and avoid forming any close relationships. Self-imposed isolation is another way to avoid being revictimized. Similar to certain Holocaust victims, many incest victims struggle with alexithymia—feeling "dead" and lacking affection or empathy for anyone. They deeply fear that the incestuous abuse has destroyed their capacity to love another person.[72] Others, by contrast, respond to their abusive past by desperately seeking attachment to others at all costs; in their desire for social approval, they tend to be "people-pleasers" and continue to project a false self that is socially acceptable to others.

In regard to romantic relationships, there is a strong tendency for many incest victims to reexperience interpersonal abuse and betrayal. The reasons for this are complex. Many incest victims report having trouble establishing safe and appropriate physical and psychological boundaries. Furthermore, they have never learned the skills of setting boundaries to protect themselves or of communicating when conflict arises. Since many victims have never witnessed or experienced healthy, loving relationships, they have obvious difficulty believing that such relationships are possible, let alone believing they are capable of cultivating them. Many resign themselves to abuse, feeling that it is inevitable in all their relationships. In addition, just as they once idealized their parents, many women tend to idealize their romantic partners in order to attain a sense of security. When their boyfriends/husbands do not live up to the idealization, these female victims reexperience intense negative emotions, if not retraumatization. Herman notes: "The survivor develops a pattern of intense, unstable relationships, repeatedly enacting dramas of rescue, injustice, and betrayal."[73] As one might expect, research studies indicate that child sexual abuse victims experience higher rates of marital problems and divorce than nonabused women.[74]

As for the capacity to relate sexually toward another person, incest victims' struggles are multiple. It is unfortunately common among many survivors to confuse sex with intimacy due to their childhood experience of only having been treated with some measure of affection during sexual abuse. Many survivors report feeling unable to integrate affection/intimacy and sexual activity. Often, they feel able to perform sexually only with persons for whom they feel no affection. Given their repeated experiences of being sexually objectified, many incest survivors may have internalized their perpetrators' attitude that their sexuality is the only worthwhile and lovable aspect of themselves. Many become promiscuous even when they experience no physical pleasure during sex, believing sex is the only way to feel valued.

Other incest victims respond in the opposite manner: they experience strong aversion to any sexual contact and have trouble tolerating any form of sexual touch, let alone pleasure.[75] In addition, they may experience flashbacks in the form of bodily memories of past abuse and suffer from severe panic and anxiety. Obviously, these forms of sexual dysfunction can negatively impact persons' degree of intimacy and satisfaction with their partners.

As for the effects of child sexual abuse on future parenting, some incest survivors are somehow able to summon the resources needed to provide their children with the healthy childhood they never experienced themselves. According to numerous research studies, however, many incest survivors manifest tremendous anxiety at the very idea of being a parent. Some purposefully avoid becoming mothers, citing the concern that they might abuse children.[76] Many incest survivors report lacking overall parenting skills, and report greater difficulty in their relationships with their children than nonabused mothers do.[77] Incest survivors who lack social support and suffer from depression and anxiety also struggle to have sufficient energy to interact with their children. Some survivors report that when relating to their children they feel detached, numb, and emotionally distant and have trouble expressing affection and even managing physical contact.[78] One survivor, for example, tape-recorded herself telling stories so that her son could listen to her voice when she could not tolerate his proximity or touch.[79] Many survivors express that care requiring greater physical intimacy, like bathing or changing diapers, can provoke great anxiety as well; the boundaries between appropriate touch and abuse are easily blurred.[80] Many incest survivors also express great fear at being unable to protect their children from potential victimization, and many react by being overprotective, which strains their relationships.[81] Sadly, this fear seems warranted: statistically, children of mothers who were sexually abused are themselves more likely to be sexually abused.[82]

As for the impact of incestuous abuse on victims' view of God and their ability to relate positively to God, most studies conducted in this underresearched area have found that child sexual abuse negatively affects female victims' conceptions of God and their perceived relationships with God.[83] Incest victims tend to perceive God as more distant toward them, as more judgmental, harsh, and/or ashamed of them than nonabused women. Such conceptions of God in turn give rise to more ambivalent or negative feelings and attitudes toward God than those held by nonabused women. Likewise, many therapists specializing in child sexual abuse report that a high percentage of sexual abuse survivors express greater fear and shame before God.[84] One woman, for instance, who was incestuously abused as a child, remained married to an abusive husband for years out of fear that God would punish her if she divorced.[85] Survivors also tend to emphasize God's judgment. Just as children resort to self-blame to justify an abusive parent's behavior, children and adult survivors alike employ the same defense mechanism to explain how a benevolent God could allow such abuse. Continuing to feel guilty about their abuse, many of these women resort to prayer and seek reparation from God to absolve them of their evil core. In their study, John Lemoncelli and Andrew Carey find that their population of sexual abuse survivors desire intimacy with God "but their perceived unworthiness prevents this from ever being experienced."[86]

Other sexual abuse survivors, having felt a profound loss of trust in and betrayal by a God who did nothing to stop the abuse, express great anger toward God. In her work *Healing the Incest Wound*, Christine Courtois asserts, "Many survivors balk at the idea of God or a higher power, feeling as though they were long ago abandoned by a cruel and uncaring God."[87] William Justice and Warren Lambert find that many survivors felt cut off "by a distant and inaccessible God."[88] Many survivors also report having trouble trusting in God's love and presence.[89] For instance, one survivor struggles with issues of abandonment, perpetually wondering whether God really exists: "I was wondering where was God when I was being abused? I mean he totally ignored me as a child."[90]

In an attempt to understand why child sexual abuse negatively impacts one's God-relationship, various psychologists have argued that a correlation exists between one's conceptions of parents and one's God image. They suggest that a child's image of God mirrors her perception of her parents.[91] Other psychologists suggest that an even stronger correlation exists between one's self-concept and one's God-concept.[92] Torre and colleagues found that among survivors of father-daughter incest, low self-esteem positively correlated with a controlling, harsh, demanding concept of God.[93] It may be that for incest survivors, the most pervasive effects of child sexual abuse—negative self-concept and low self-esteem—in turn threaten survivors' ability to relate with trust and love to God.

Conclusion

This chapter has attempted to convey the profoundly insidious effects of child sexual abuse on one's developing sense of self and one's capacity for relationality and autonomy. At this point, we turn to examine certain feminist theories of self and agency that provide points of contrast with Rahner's theological anthropology. These alternative positions offer valuable theoretical insights that illuminate the experiences of traumatization, thus offering suggestions for a revised Rahnerian theology of freedom that will resonate with trauma survivors' experiences.

4

The Fragmented Self and Constrained Agency

Feminist Theories as Correctives to a Rahnerian Anthropology

Before analyzing how trauma theory challenges the adequacy of Rahner's account of the self, freedom, and God's grace, I wish to compare his theological anthropology to contemporary feminist accounts of subjectivity and freedom. Examining alternative understandings of self and freedom will offer points of contrast to Rahner's theological anthropology. Ultimately, this will give us a more comprehensive viewpoint from which to evaluate whether Rahner's theology has the resources to attend adequately to the realities of trauma victims and empower them in their process of recovery. Perhaps a particular feminist understanding of the self and agency is better equipped to address the challenges of trauma theory than Rahner's. If this were the case, it would be more fruitful to incorporate an entirely different perspective on subjectivity and agency into our theological reflections on trauma victims rather than seeking to revise Rahner's theology. After analyzing certain feminist theories of the self and freedom, I argue that both Rahner's and feminist conceptions of the self and freedom present us with positive insights as well as limitations when we seek to reflect theologically on the experiences of trauma victims; consequently, my objective is to incorporate certain insights from both accounts when constructing a revised theology of freedom.

There are many contemporary philosophical accounts of subjectivity and agency that could serve as valuable conversation partners for Rahner and trauma theory. My primary reason for focusing on feminist accounts of the self and freedom is as follows: since this book examines the suffering and oppression of a particular group of girls and women, it seems reasonable to explore whether feminist theories—united in their concern with the liberation and well-being of women—are more responsive to the experiences of trauma victims than Rahner's theological anthropology. The contested meaning of autonomy and self-determination in feminist theory notwithstanding, a key objective for women's liberation and flourishing has consistently been the realization of some form of autonomy—some sense of taking control and responsibility for one's life. In this way, although their particular accounts of freedom might differ, many feminists share with Rahner a commitment to the importance of agency for human flourishing. Compared with Rahner, however, feminist theorists have analyzed in greater depth the ways that oppressive forms of socialization and acts of violence directed toward women and others (rape, domestic violence, etc.) have obstructed the effective development of a positive sense of self and autonomy. Some feminists have even questioned how, given the profoundly damaging nature of oppression, oppressed persons can be thought to be agents at all.[1] Since it is likely that their analysis of the effects of oppression may parallel studies of certain effects of trauma, the objective of this chapter is to see if a feminist analysis of sexist oppression offers a reservoir of insights for a revised theology of freedom, one that can speak to trauma victims' experiences.

I will examine the views of two feminist theorists, Judith Butler and Diana Meyers. I choose these philosophers because they represent two distinctive representative positions on the self and agency within the spectrum of current feminist theory. First, I analyze Butler's poststructuralist account of the self and agency, since it presents a radically different account of subjectivity and agency than Rahner's theological anthropology. Many feminist theologians find her poststructuralist account of the self to be the only feasible option for constructive theological reflection in general.[2] Butler has been at the forefront of feminist theory, problematizing long-held assumptions about sex, gender, and the relationship between discourse and the materiality of the body. Because it is difficult to overestimate Butler's influence on feminist theory and theology, I will narrow my consideration of poststructuralist feminist theory to her representative position.

Second, I examine Diana Meyers's feminist account of the self and autonomy, which offers a strikingly different view from Butler's. Like Rahner, Meyers affirms the importance of persons' capacity for self-determination and an integrated sense of self. As we will see, however, unlike Rahner, she dismisses the need to address the issue of free will and focuses solely on a procedural account of the process of self-determination. Meyers's approach to autonomy suggests that a revised theological account of freedom better serves the needs of trauma victims, as long as it remains neutral on the free will/determinism debate and focuses descriptively only on how autonomy can be fostered.

After examining these feminist conceptions of self and agency and noting their differences from Rahner's, I will identify ways they both succeed and fail to offer theoretical insights that shed light on the victimization and potential recovery of incestuously abused women.

Butler's Conception of the Self

Judith Butler rejects modernist conceptions of the self as an autonomous agent who wills and effectively carries out intentions through actions. She argues that the self does not possess any inherent structures or "natural" attributes that underlie a "true" self. The so-called universal capacities for reason, language, moral deliberation, and free will are instead purely contingent: "There is no ontologically intact reflexivity to the subject which is then placed within a cultural context."[3] Accordingly, Butler is in direct opposition to Rahner's idea that certain existentials (transcendentality, subjectivity, freedom and responsibility for self-determination, and God's ever-present self-offer—the supernatural existential) are given and hence define what it means to be human. Butler would undoubtedly argue that, far from expressing any necessary "truth" about the human condition, Rahner's existentials are merely contingent on the cultural discourses of his historical time and place.

Proposing a poststructuralist conception of the self, Butler argues that there is no subjectivity except that which is constituted by the "discursive and social relations" of one's culture.[4] Subjectivity in poststructuralist theory generally refers to "the conscious and unconscious thoughts and emotions of the individual, her sense of herself and her ways of understanding her relation to the world."[5] The subject is constituted or comes to be, only as "a consequence of certain rules-governed discourses that govern the intelligible invocation of identity."[6] These discourses consist of not only linguistic narratives about the self and world but also our social practices and institutional arrangements. One's sense of self—one's very identity—is constructed and formed throughout a process of relating to others within the reigning power-discourse matrices of a given society: "What the person 'is' is always relative to the constructed relations in which it is determined."[7]

For Butler, it is impossible to step "outside" the relations of power if one wishes to communicate in ways that are socially intelligible to others. She compares persons' repetitive enactments of socially acceptable gestures, conventions, and norms to the performances of an actor: "The act that one does, the act that one performs, is, in a sense, an act that has been going on before one arrived on the scene."[8] Thus, Butler argues that "there is no being behind doing, expecting, becoming; 'the doer' is merely a fiction added to the deed—the deed is everything."[9] The self as "doer" is constructed "in and through the deed."[10] Such a claim will be very significant when we analyze her theory of agency below.

Comparing Butler's self-as-constituted-through-the-deed to Rahner's subject, it is important to recognize that Rahner's self is constituted through actions as well. In each case, one's free actions shape and ultimately constitute the self one becomes throughout one's lifetime. For Rahner, however, there is a normative conception of what constitutes "authentic" selfhood and fulfillment; there are certain capacities that are given within the structure of what it means to be a person—for example, capacities to know, to love, and to choose. These await actualization and fulfillment, but a direction is set. Rahner argues that, despite all the ways that discourses and relations determine the self, the self has freedom to choose how to respond to each situation. Ultimately, there are only two possible fundamental choices for the emerging self: to accept God's self-offer and experience true fulfillment in communion with the divine, or to reject God and experience eternal dissatisfaction. Essentially, what constitutes the measure of the "true self" is determined by God.

In contrast, Butler's meaning of the self's authenticity and fulfillment is fluid, absolutely contingent on the reigning historical and cultural discourses of one's time. In her theory of identity formation, the relationship between language, subjectivity, and meaning is the reverse of what is found in Rahner. For Rahner, the self employs language to express and describe objective truths about human nature and the rest of reality; persons possess original prethematic knowledge that they obtain from experience and only then seek to conceptualize in order to communicate with others. One's subjective consciousness gives one access to truth and meaning. It is thus possible to attain closer and closer approximations of truth, defined as representing the "real."

For Butler, on the other hand, language exists prior to the existence of subjectivity and establishes the parameters of our understanding of the self, as well as the rest of human reality. Furthermore, there is no way to "get outside" the present discourses of one's society to apprehend reality "out there."[11] There is nothing, including the materiality of the body, that is prior to discursive relations: "That the gendered body is performative suggests that it has no ontological status apart from the various acts which constitute its reality."[12] Butler refers to the body as a cultural situation, as a "field of cultural possibilities both received and reinterpreted."[13]

Such claims that the body has no ontological status apart from its various acts has prompted critics to accuse Butler of linguistic monism, a radical constructivist position affirming that language exhaustively constitutes matter. In her work *Bodies That Matter,* Butler assures her readers that she does not believe words alone have "the power to craft bodies from their own linguistic substance."[14] She grants that bodies live and die and experience pain, pleasure, illness, and violence. However, she asserts that the irrefutability of these "facts" "in no way implies what it might mean to affirm them and through what discursive means."[15] Butler rejects the move to appeal to any "bodily facts" when advancing normative claims. Any claim we make about the body is not merely descriptive but functions performatively,[16] because the materiality of the body and the rest of reality is inescapably coconstructed by discourse: "There is no reference to a pure body which is not at the same time a further formation of that body."[17] The upshot is that, even though Butler acknowledges that language does not exhaust ontological reality, it is only our discursive construal of reality that constitutes "*that which is significant,* that which 'matters' to the human interpreter."[18]

Finally, Butler parts ways with modern thinkers when she questions the significance and legitimacy of common philosophical concerns about self-continuity and self-coherence. She argues that these concepts are, in fact, ideals we hold about the self rather than actual descriptions of our lived experience as selves possessing an identity.[19] She asks: "What grounds the presumption that identities are self-identical, persisting through time as the same, unified and internally coherent?"[20] Rather than praising the human capacity for self-coherence and self-continuity, Butler argues that repeated performances and actions give rise to the *illusion* of coherency and stability in identity. Wishing to subvert hegemonic social practices and expectations, she celebrates instead the possibility of fragmentation of identity and the possibility of change. Such affirmation of fragmentation conflicts with a modernist conception of a self who is striving for integration. While Rahner would agree with Butler that persons experience conflicting desires that threaten them from establishing a coherent sense of self over time, he would find nothing to celebrate about this condition, for it is due (in his view) to distorted desires and sin. After all, the goal of human life for Rahner is to integrate all of one's desires and fragments into an identity united in love for God and neighbor.

Butler's View of Agency

Finding the modernist concept of agency untenable, Butler consistently rejects the view of a self who, endowed with free will, expresses "his" intentions through language and action. For Butler, agency is not a universal attribute that all humans possess by virtue of their reason; neither is it a "capacity for reflexive mediation that remains intact regardless of its cultural embeddedness."[21] Instead of taking agency for granted as an a priori guarantee or existential that is constitutive of human life, Butler argues that it is "crucial to question the conditions of its possibility."[22] Agency is embedded within complex matrices of power and discourse and is "always and only a political prerogative."[23]

Responding to criticisms that a completely discursively constituted self eliminates agency and therefore hope for transformative change and liberation, Butler emphatically states that the constituted self is by no means determined: "The constituted character of the subject is the very precondition of its agency."[24] Why is this the case? Butler claims that the act of being constituted as a subject is a never-ending process. The condition for the possibility of agency is found in the very process of reenacting and reiterating the discursive/social practices that constitute a human subject: agency is a "double-movement of being constituted in and by a signifier, where 'to be constituted' means 'to be compelled to cite or repeat or mime' the signifier itself."[25] She describes the self as a "site" of complex, often competing power discourses. It is due to this complexity and instability of the site of discourses that agency construed as resistance against hegemonic power is possible. While repetitive actions can reify the dominant social conventions, slight variations in performative recitations can also serve to subvert and destabilize them: "Agency is to be found precisely at such junctures where discourse is renewed."[26] By working within the confines and laws of already existing relations of power-discourses, it is possible to resignify and rework these discourses, finding new convergences among them. Agency, then, is more properly an "effect" of discursive conditions than the cause of subsequent action. According to Butler, the subject is "the permanent possibility of a certain resignifying process, one which gets detoured and stalled through other mechanisms of power, but which is power's own possibility of being reworked."[27]

Depicting agency as an effect of new discursive possibilities raises the following question. What in Butler's view precisely motivates subversion, the variations in repetitive performances, the "resignifying of the signifying"? What causes persons to engage in parodic performances that subvert dominant discourses rather than reify them? Are such variations accidental or are they intentional on the part of subjects? And is the effect of shifting practices the genuine emergence of a self engaging meaningfully in some degree of self-determination, or simply permutations in social processes that offer new constructions for the nominal subject?

Throughout many of her writings, Butler's stance on all of this appears to be one of ambivalence. As Lise Nelson observes, Butler construes agency in *Gender Trouble* as arising through new discursive possibilities; subversion occurs when competing discourses accidentally converge in different ways to produce new possibilities.[28] For instance, Butler says, "Discourses present themselves in the plural, coexisting within temporal frames, and instituting unpredictable and inadvertent convergences from which specific modalities of discursive possibilities are engendered."[29] In *Feminist Contentions*, Butler continues to emphasize that change and manifestations of agency are not due to critical consciousness or intentionality on the part of subjects. Consider three key claims:

> The deed will be itself and the legacy of conventions that it opens up; the doer will be the uncertain working of discursive possibilities by which it itself is worked.[30]
>
> To the extent that a performative appears to "express" a prior intention, a doer *behind* the deed, that prior agency is only legible *as the effect* of that utterance. For a performative to work, it must draw upon and recite a set of linguistic conventions which have traditionally worked to bind or engage certain kinds of effects.[31]
>
> When words engage actions or constitute themselves a kind of action, this is not because they reflect the power of an individual's will or intention, but because they draw upon and reengage conventions which have gained their power precisely through a sedimented iterability.[32]

At times, then, Butler implies that any appearance of a person seeking to express intentions through action is just that—an appearance. Note how Butler constructs an antithesis between the modern conception of agency as an ontological attribute of an autonomous, already fully self-determining rational self, and her own construal of agency as arising from unintentional variations in discursive repetitions without reliance on the intentions of subjects. Presuming the inevitability of this sharp dichotomy, Butler finds the latter more persuasive.

Despite Butler's insistence on severing the concept of agency from any construal of the subjective consciousness of persons in these works, it is questionable whether she actually follows through consistently with this claim. In fact, in *Gender Trouble*, *Bodies That Matter*, and *Feminist Contentions*, Butler implicitly presumes the exercise of critical capacities in the process of subversion, resignification, and resistance.[33] Consider, for instance, the following. "My position is mine to the extent that I replay and resignify the theoretical positions that have constituted me, working the possibilities of their convergence, and trying to take account of the possibilities that they systematically exclude."[34] In this text, Butler invokes the image of a person critically reflecting on all the discourses that have constituted her as she creatively thinks of new discursive convergences that will intentionally subvert dominant discourses about identity. As Vasterling and Nelson point out, Butler also uses phrases such as "self-critical," "dispute," "critical reflection," "laying claim to terms," and being "formed by [power] as one reworks it." Such language presumes an intentional, self-reflexive person who is capable of action, which bears remarkable resemblance to the modernist subject so excoriated by Butler.[35]

In her later work *The Psychic Life of Power*, Butler seeks to revise her account of subjectivity and agency, addressing criticisms that she does not adequately account for how subjects become motivated to destabilize and resist hegemonic discourses. Her objective is to theorize about the process of subjection in which one becomes subordinated by power in the process of emerging as a subject. She seeks to offer an adequate account of subjection and elucidate how such a conception of the subject can "work as a notion of political agency in postliberatory times."[36] Expressing dissatisfaction that Foucault's construal of discursive power cannot sufficiently account for how resistance to reigning power discourses is possible,[37] Butler seeks to conjoin Foucault's theory of power with Freud's theory of the psyche.[38] Butler argues that, throughout the process of subjection in which power presses the subject into subordination, the subject becomes attached to the conditions of subordination: "To desire the conditions of one's own subordination is thus required to persist as one's self."[39] Subjects need to repeatedly reenact and recite cultural conventions and norms that preceded their existence in order to be socially recognized as a subject. Consistent with her earlier works, Butler accounts for agency through her theory of performativity: subjects' recitations and reiterations can destabilize and subvert the meaning and purposes of hegemonic power:

> What is enacted by the subject is enabled but not finally constrained by the prior working of power. Agency exceeds the power by which it is enabled. One might say that the purposes of power are not always the purposes of agency. . . . Agency is the assumption of a purpose unintended by power, one that could not have been derived logically or historically, that operates the relation of contingency and reversal to the power that makes it possible, to which it nevertheless belongs.[40]

While Butler seems to link agency explicitly with a subject's intentionality more closely than in her previous works, it is highly questionable whether her appropriation of Freud's theory of the psyche accounts any better for subjects' motivation to resist hegemonic social norms.[41] As Catherine Mills argues, claiming that agency is dependent on the subject's desire for conditions of subordination actually seems to create further obstacles when explaining why a subject would be inspired to resist and seek social transformation if the possible risk is social and perhaps actual death.[42] It still remains unclear why agency, according to Butler, "exceeds the power by which it is enabled," and why subjects would wish to subvert the purposes intended by power, especially if they have become passionately attached to the dynamics of subordination.

Evaluating Butler's Poststructuralist Self in the Context of Trauma

Given this review of Butler's theory of subjectivity and agency, it is now possible to explore whether such a theory provides a fruitful approach to trauma victims' experiences of both traumatization and the process of recovery. There are, indeed, at least three advantages to Butler's poststructuralist theory over a modernist framework as it relates to trauma victims.

First, among the positive ramifications, Butler's performativity theory avoids certain problems that arise in many modern accounts of subjectivity and freedom. Since poststructuralism denies that there are innate attributes of the self that exist prior to discourse and experience, it avoids the danger of presupposing that freedom for self-determination follows necessarily from an ability to reason. In addition, by not assuming freedom as an ontological attribute, poststructuralism avoids the societal tendency to blame victims for not preventing their own traumatic reenactments, which often take the form of self-destructive actions and repeated revictimization. Butler's philosophy, then, resonates with experiences of trauma victims by suggesting that neither adequate subjectivity nor a capacity for free control over emotions and actions can be taken for granted as "givens" lodged in the nature of members of the human species.

Second, the poststructuralist conception of how discourses constitute the self clearly sheds light on how the high prevalence of child sexual abuse is possible in American society. An array of discourses form and shape perpetrators' and others' perceptions of children as both vulnerable and sexual, as well as disempower children from developing a sufficient sense of agency to defend their bodily integrity. Innumerable discourses also converge to exacerbate the effects of incest and contribute to subsequent posttraumatic symptoms identified with sexual abuse: examples of such discourses include social practices that make fathers unquestioned "heads of the household," discourses that discourage children from revealing the abuse, lack of effective social institutions to protect children, laws that often protect perpetrators, discourses that attack recovered memories of abuse, and so on. Poststructuralism thus accounts for the ways discourses help construct and enable the epidemic of child sexual abuse in American society.

Third, Butler's poststructuralist theory helps explain why it is so difficult to dislodge the discourses and practices that constitute a person even when one recognizes their harmful effects. In *The Psychic Life of Power*, Butler briefly mentions the problem of child sexual abuse. She analyzes how children are not merely exploited in the sense that an adult unilaterally imposes sexual activity on the child; a child's passionate love and attachment to an adult, which is necessary for survival, is abused and exploited, and this fusion of love and abuse has psychic effects.[43] As Butler notes: "It is clearly not the case that 'I' preside over the positions that have constituted me, shuffling through them instrumentally, casting some aside, incorporating others, although some of my activity may take that form. The 'I' who would select between them is always already constituted by them."[44] In other words, because a trauma victim is wholly constituted by social discourses, not merely situated in and influenced by them, it is not possible for her (or anyone else) simply to recognize certain discourses and practices as harmful and then effectively dismiss them in such a way that they exert no further influence. If this were possible, recovery from traumatization would be a smooth and assured cognitive process of simply casting aside negative discourses and adopting more positive ones that give birth to a new subject with a positive self-concept. Butler thus helps us understand why a victim can be both overwhelmed and "reconstituted" by abuse, and why recovery from chronic, interpersonal harm is such an arduous process.

When we move to the issue of what enables the possibility of recovery, however, we also begin to see the limitations of Butler's conceptions of self and agency. What makes possible the constructive changes that lead to recovery? Butler's answer is that competing discourses destabilize the subject and account for such change. Unfortunately, this reply only takes us so far. For instance, it leaves us with the image of an incest victim who is confronted with a bewildering array of conflicting discourses that offer alternative interpretations of the abuse and her self-concept. And yet, being at this site of destabilizing discourses does not adequately account for what makes positive changes possible in the life of any concrete person. What enables the next choice, decision, or action for persons who are at this destabilizing site of competing discourses? Why, for instance, is one incest victim able to negotiate social discourses in such a way that she overcomes self-destructive behaviors while another struggles with the same competing discourses for years, only to commit suicide? Is it all a matter of luck or contingency in the river of competing discourses?

Butler's conception of the self as constituted by discourse, as the "consequence of rules-governed practices," does not allow her to grapple sufficiently with the complexity that occurs when trauma victims negotiate and struggle with the conflicting discourses that are vying for their allegiance. Although Butler asserts that the constituted self is not determined, it is unclear why this is the case. The most she can say is the following: "The subject is not determined by the rules through which it is generated because signification is not a founding act, but rather a regulated process of repetition."[45] And yet, she fails to explain how a "regulated process of repetition" avoids determinism, and how this narrowed construal of agency depicted as resistance is finally helpful to concrete subjects, such as sexual abuse survivors and those who support them in the process of recovery. Butler's philosophical position thus leaves her unable to account for the process in which an actual trauma victim chooses one option over another at a particular point in time.

Butler's claim that agency is an effect of discourse rather than a capacity of persons also prevents her from identifying concrete abilities that enable trauma victims to negotiate among the competing discourses and make constructive changes in their lives. Claiming that change occurs during accidental variations in repetitive performances hardly offers any hope or useful insights for incest victims to overcome their compulsion to reenact the trauma and choose positive options that lead to healing. According to the actual experiences of trauma victims, key abilities that enable overcoming self-destructive behaviors include learning how to trust and connect with others,[46] developing the capacity to reflect on past experiences of abuse and how it has affected their lives, being receptive to feedback from others, and being able to imagine new possibilities. As discussed earlier, Butler's account of agency fails to acknowledge the significance of these conscious capacities, presumably out of fear that such acknowledgment will reintroduce the self-determining Enlightenment subject.

In addition, Butler's version of constructivism fails to theorize adequately about the best way to foster recovery precisely because it celebrates fragmentation of the self and devalues the importance of capacities that, according to trauma theorists, are essential for recovery from traumatization. As noted, Butler questions the importance of valuing and possessing self-continuity and self-coherency, and she rejects any notion of agency that is explicitly related to the intentions of subjects. In sharp contrast, trauma survivors find that developing a sense of self-continuity and self-coherency as well as a sense of effective agency is crucial for recovery and full reengagement with daily life.[47] Butler appears to ignore the psychological need persons have for some sense of coherency. The root cause of this, perhaps, is her failure to distinguish between the absolutely unified, encapsulated Enlightenment self and the minimal sense of self-coherency necessary for any kind of purposive action. The psychoanalyst Jane Flax's criticism of postmodern philosophers' exaggerated praise for fragmentation appropriately applies to Butler:

> Borderline patients lack a core self without which the registering of and pleasure in a variety of experiencing of ourselves, others, and the outer world are simply not possible. Those who celebrate or call for a "decentered" self seem self-deceptively naive and unaware of the basic cohesion within themselves that makes the fragmentation of experiences something other than a terrifying slide into psychosis.[48]

Thus, Flax argues that underlying postmodern philosophers' celebrated experience of fragmentation is actually a minimal core sense of self. Besides the fact that Butler romanticizes a state of mind that in actuality causes severe suffering and incapacitation, her move to devalue self-coherency and self-continuity and reject any notion of conscious agency fails to offer any constructive guidance on how to effect liberating changes at the concrete level of persons' lives, let alone how to assist trauma victims in recovery.

Yet Butler need not ignore altogether a desire for self-coherency. Imagine, for instance, how she might directly converse with trauma victims who desperately long for a coherent sense of self and some control over their actions and emotions. Far from describing the perceived needs of trauma victims in ways likely to offend or disempower, she could explain them more sympathetically as values directly derived from dominant Western social discourses. She would not thereby be committed to an account of the self who inherently possesses certain fixed psychological needs and characteristics, and nevertheless her words might still resonate with trauma victims' experiences.

While Butler's constructivism does not necessarily lead to a trivialization of trauma survivors' needs for self-coherency and self-continuity, her claim about the utter contingency of these needs is neither self-evident nor helpful. Is it compelling to claim that these desires for self-coherency, self-continuity, and the ability to exert some control over the direction of one's life are completely constructed by existing dominant discourses? It does not seem feasible to maintain that the opposite state of affairs—absolute fragmentation of the self, lack of memories about one's past, and an almost complete lack of control over one's emotions and actions—may be considered optimal psychological functioning as long as our social discourses espouse such values. In the end, the actual suffering of innumerable incest victims who struggle with fragmented selves and lack of agency challenge Butler's view that the attributes necessary for developing a constructive sense of self and healthy psychological functioning are unilaterally constructed by reigning social discourses.

Butler's poststructuralist constructivism has at least one remaining major flaw that is related to her construal of the relation between language, materiality, and subjectivity. If we take seriously her claim that the materiality of bodies is coconstructed by discourse, it follows that what constitutes harm to bodies is similarly constructed and hence contingent upon existing social discourses. Applying the issue of child sexual abuse to Butler's argument that any "description" of the body is a further formation of that body, it becomes clear that her position may undermine the claim that sexual intercourse with children constitutes exploitation and violation regardless of the particular social discourses of a given family, community, or society. If discourses form and construct our knowledge and experiences of our bodies, Butler's constructivist position must be open in theory to the possibility that actions like having intercourse with a five-year-old and selling one's child into prostitution can promote healthy physical and psychosocial development as long as the reigning social discourses support the idea that these practices are good for children's well-being.

At this point, it is appropriate to criticize the extent to which Butler views bodies as fluid and amenable to further formation through discourses. Does not the materiality of the body—irrespective of our discourses about such materiality—impose limits on the credibility of discourses about conditions needed for children's physical and psychological well-being? If the materiality of the body does condition and circumscribe our perceptions of which discourses are credible and compelling, this undermines Butler's poststructuralist position that language unilaterally constitutes what we can know about the materiality of the body. According to Butler, language is the "very condition" under which materiality and the rest of reality may be said to appear.[49]

Trauma research on child sexual abuse challenges this unilateral construal of the relation between language, materiality, and subjectivity.[50] Violent action done to bodies—for instance, sexual intercourse with a five-year-old—severely impacts a child's experience of embodiment and her developing subjectivity. Interestingly, this is especially the case when sexual abuse overwhelms a child's ability to register the abuse consciously and comprehend what is occurring. As we have seen, many children who dissociate completely during sexual abuse nevertheless bear its marks by experiencing a host of associated symptoms and disorders. The fact that such traumatic events, which are extralinguistic, unspeakable, and not discursively assimilated into a child's overall understanding of reality, have the power to impact subjectivity and embodiment so pervasively strongly demonstrates that Butler's account of the discursive process of becoming a subject is incomplete. In addition to the idea that social discourses constitute subjects, child sexual abuse research indicates that what actually happens to bodies—regardless of what a subject consciously comprehends—affects one's developing subjectivity. Researchers identify two factors in particular that greatly determine the severity of traumatization arising from sexual abuse: (1) the severity of sexual abuse in terms of the specific sexual activity and (2) the degree of physical force or violence used in the abuse.[51] The more intrusive the sexual activity and the greater the violence involved in the sexual abuse, the more severe the posttraumatic symptoms.[52] These factors, along with research about the neurobiological and physiological changes resulting from child sexual abuse, suggest that it is not solely our cultural discourses that inform and shape a child's reaction to sexual abuse; something about our bodily constitution makes us vulnerable to pain and violation, dissociation and traumatization. If this is true, bodily responses to sexual abuse limit the scope of credible discourses about human bodies and what constitutes bodily well-being.[53]

Butler neglects to acknowledge the idea that the materiality of the body dynamically impacts our discourses because it contradicts her epistemological stance that we can only know what is discursively constructed. Her construal of the relation between discourses and the materiality of the body robs her of any resources to make normative claims to the effect that intrusive sexual activity constitutes violence and harm universally to children because she explicitly rejects the idea that there is something about the materiality of bodies that can ground or verify a set of injuries or violations.[54] Throughout her works, Butler rejects the move to advance universal norms or values on the grounds that they are oppressive and exclusionary.[55]

Thus, Butler's unilateral depiction of discourses coconstructing the materiality of bodies ultimately implies that whatever constitutes violence and harm is contingent on social discourse. However, as I have shown, this position relativizes too far the meaning of violence and abuse, and can be used to legitimate the views of adults in our society who condone sexual activity with children.[56] Clearly, constructivist arguments like Butler's could easily be used to minimize the harmful effects of child sexual abuse, ultimately undermining our society's already weak resolve to prevent child sexual abuse and punish perpetrators.[57] Given the vast research documenting the traumatization of incest victims whose perpetrators often defended their acts of sexual violence, it is evident that intrusive sexual activity constitutes violation and harm regardless of the surrounding social discourses.

To conclude, then, Butler's poststructuralist theory fails to offer an adequate account of persons' lived experiences of subjectivity and agency, and it neglects to offer insights about how best to promote human well-being, including healing and recovery for trauma victims. Her radical constructivism may be effective in deconstructing the privileged identities of heterosexual persons who enjoy what is otherwise thought to be a normal, "natural" status. However, when it comes to a theory of identity for marginalized and severely traumatized persons whose need is precisely a minimally coherent sense of self, Butler's poststructuralist project falls short. For those theologians who wish to continue making normative judgments about what violates persons' well-being and what promotes their flourishing, this analysis of Butler's work should caution them from fully embracing a poststructuralist account of the self and agency.

This does not mean, of course, that a constructivist account of the self and agency has no value for understanding trauma. Its usefulness may be clearer if we interpret it in a weak sense. That is, we can agree with Butler that social discourses and practices significantly constitute subjects—certainly more pervasively than Rahner acknowledges—without concluding that all aspects of the human person are thereby exhaustively constituted. We can also embrace Butler's position that effective agency is not an invulnerable, already actualized ontological attribute. We must indeed identify conditions that make agency possible, but we need not join Butler in the further rejection of viewing agency as a capacity that persons can realize within a context of supportive relations.

To attain greater insight about how to develop this ability to exercise effective agency, it is helpful to turn to the work of another feminist philosopher, Diana Meyers.

Meyers's Account of Autonomy and the Authentic Self

Diana Meyers shares Butler's view that the self is socially constructed and that agency cannot be presumed as a given ontological attribute. However, these similarities can be misleading. Unlike Butler, Meyers finds it crucial to conceive of agency—or "autonomy," as she prefers—as a capacity. Like Rahner, she considers the capacity for self-determination to be central to human fulfillment, and argues that social conditions thwarting the realization of this capacity constitute injustice and grave harm. In her work *Self, Society, and Personal Choice,* Meyers's objective is to offer a procedural account of autonomy that elucidates how a person can discern what she really wants and develop a life plan of "her own." Defending the very idea of autonomy is challenging, she argues, since the social sciences have made us more aware than ever before of the profound extent to which selves are socially constructed. Such awareness calls into question whether a person's characteristics, beliefs, interests, and ideals can be credibly referred to as "her own":

> If people are products of their environments, it seems fatuous to maintain that the agency of individuals has any special importance, for personal choice dissolves into social influence. Moreover, it seems vacuous to maintain that there is a significant distinction between what a person wants and what that person really wants, for people have no desires apart from those that socialization has molded, if not implanted in them.[58]

In response to this challenge to the very notion of autonomy, Meyers looks to claims by contemporary philosophers who have sought to "rescue" autonomy from socialization.[59] She analyzes three of these accounts in particular. The first, advanced by the philosopher Robert Young, examines the socialization process of any self in order to see whether anyone can be freed at least from negative socialization. Young argues that socialization can cease to be coercive and to threaten autonomy if the unconscious shaping forces are rendered explicit at the conscious level.[60] The second account, proposed by Stanley Benn, focuses on using one's critical faculties to attain coherency with respect to one's beliefs and values. The third account, formulated by Harry Frankfurt, focuses on the decision to identify with certain traits, desires, and values, and to act consistently in accordance with them.

Meyers is deeply critical of these accounts of autonomy, arguing that their main problem is their reduction of autonomy to the ontological issue of free will. Their primary concern, she claims, is to explain how a person's authentic self can transcend the effects of socialization: "Young maintains that knowledge sets us free; Benn maintains that coherency sets us free; Frankfurt maintains that deciding sets us free."[61] Meyers finds it problematic that such accounts essentially view the "true" self as buried innately within a person as if it were a sunken treasure: the only way to discover the self is to utilize one's free will and shed all the layers of socialization that have buried it. She questions the kind of autonomy this self possesses, charging that such "freedom" is fatalistic. Under such a conception, freedom consists solely in the life task of discovering an innate, transcendent self and dutifully acting in accordance with its directives. According to Meyers, this view of freedom lacks an appreciation for the phenomenon of self-definition, which consists of establishing one's personal standards and forming a sense of the kind of person one desires to become.

If asked to evaluate Rahner's conception of the self and freedom, Meyers would likely argue that his account conforms perfectly to the problematic view of autonomy conceived primarily as an issue of free will. Meyers might contend that, even though Rahner acknowledges that the self is fundamentally a social and historical being, he still falls into the trap of viewing freedom as the ability to transcend socialization. His general affirmation of persons possessing a transcendental core freedom for ultimate self-disposal, a core that is not completely vulnerable to any degree of oppressive socialization, most clearly demonstrates this. Similarly, Meyers would likely perceive Rahner's conception of freedom as fatalistic, since he espouses a "true" self who needs to accept God's self-offer in order to experience fulfillment. In Meyers's view, if Rahner is right and freedom consists in saying yes to God and actualizing one's true self (which consists of dedicating one's life to love for God and neighbor), then persons are not actually free to establish their own standards but must submit to God's conception of the "authentic self."

For Meyers, such a conception of an autonomous self capable of transcending socialization fails to be compelling. Contending that these philosophical accounts do not take seriously the degree to which socialization fosters or hinders persons' capacity to realize their autonomy, Meyers suggests it is possible to make important philosophical progress in understanding the phenomena of autonomy and self-determination by "circumventing" the ontological problem of free will altogether. She proposes that autonomy should be understood as simply the ability to be in control over one's life; an autonomous person is able to discern correctly what she "really" values and wants out of life. To be in control, then, means that one is able to "live in harmony with one's true—one's authentic—self."[62] But, as we will see, one's authentic self is not given a priori. Rather, it emerges gradually as one develops skills needed for autonomy.

Arguing that the main problem for a theory of autonomy is to explain how autonomous decisions are made, Meyers focuses solely on developing a procedural account of autonomy. In other words, the criteria for determining the autonomy of a person's decision and consequent action rest solely on the *process* through which that person makes decisions. Autonomy is thus conceived as "the exercise of a competency comprising diverse self-reading and self-actualizing skills."[63] Rather than viewing autonomy as an all-or-nothing possession, Meyers proposes that persons possess varying degrees of autonomy as they develop the skills involved in three key areas: (1) self-knowledge, which consists in having the skills to reflect on who one is and who one wishes to become; (2) self-definition, which involves being able to establish personal standards and ideals and being able to alter one's character traits to attain these standards; and (3) self-direction, which is the capacity to "express one's personality in action."[64] According to Meyers, an adequate level of autonomy skills enables persons to formulate a life plan consisting of an overarching sense of one's values, goals, priorities, and ideals. Persons must develop the skills needed to ask "What do I really want, need, care about, and value?" Second, they must have the ability to follow through by acting in accordance with their decisions. Thus, one can distinguish authentic as opposed to heteronomous desires imposed by society solely by analyzing the ways one comes to embrace and act on those values. If one has adequate knowledge of who one is, is conscious of one's values and goals, and is capable of acting to realize such goals, one can assume that one's desires are autonomous, and that one is leading an autonomous rather than a heteronomous life. For Meyers, the difference between these lives is "between feeling in control and right in your skin, on the one hand, and feeling at sea and ill at ease, on the other."[65] In short, autonomous persons are in touch with what matters most to them in life. They possess a sense that they are in charge of directing their own lives rather than being led by others' standards and expectations.

It is important to note that, in her own account of autonomy, Meyers rejects other thinkers' assumption that the "true" self precedes the exercise of freedom. In the three philosophical accounts Meyers rejects, freedom is used to uncover an enduring "true" self that has been threatened by socialization. Similarly, for Rahner, freedom enables one to respond to God's grace and become the "true" self God ordained one to be. In contrast, Meyers argues that the authentic self emerges *from* the exercise of autonomy skills. She views the authentic self as dynamic and continuously evolving: as an autonomous person successfully engages in self-knowledge, self-definition, and self-direction, he or she affirms traits and characteristics that gradually become incorporated into his or her "authentic" self. The authentic self is not fixed, but is an "evolving collocation of traits that emerges when someone exercises autonomy competency."[66] Autonomy skills are so crucial precisely because persons are shaping their selves through their daily choices and actions. Moreover, the overriding purpose of developing autonomy competency is ultimately to acquire an integrated personality. Rather than experiencing compartmentalization and serious conflicts regarding one's identity and life plan, a person with an integrated self experiences a sense of coherency among her traits and is able to direct her life according to authentic desires and goals. To Meyers, this kind of self is preferable to a fragmented, conflicted self who often suffers from profound senses of inefficacy, chronic regret, and dissatisfaction. On this issue, Meyers is in agreement with Rahner about the desirability of an integrated identity, and she sharply disagrees with Butler's celebration of fragmentation.

Meyers adds to her account the recognition that an autonomous person's self-concept and life plan mutually inform and alter one another throughout the course of his or her life. Consequently, an autonomous person's life plan is not rigid and inflexible, nor is it ever fully articulated. Skills of self-introspection allow one to be attuned to experiences of dissatisfaction regarding one's self-concept, values, and goals. When such dissatisfaction occurs, other autonomy skills help persons adjust their life plans and/or alter who they are becoming. Meyers even leaves open the possibility that radically changing one's priorities and the direction of one's life can be consistent with leading an autonomous life, as long as such decisive changes emerge from using one's autonomy skills. In general, then, autonomous persons exhibit flexibility in regard to their life course and "exercise skills that maintain a fluid interaction between their traits, their feelings, their beliefs, their values, their extended plans, their current possibilities for realizing these plans, and their conduct."[67] Consequently, autonomous persons do not experience a chronic sense of regret or unhappiness, since such states presume that one has been unable to act in accordance with one's values and goals.

When comparing her own procedural account of autonomy to the philosophical accounts described earlier, Meyers asserts that she successfully avoids the free will debate and its emphasis on escaping socialization. Her view of autonomy "is not only compatible with the civilized influences of socialization, but it depends on socialization to cultivate the requisite skills."[68] While Meyers grants that persons are born with the potentiality for autonomy and other competencies, she insists that socialization and supportive relationships with others are necessary to enable persons to transform these potentialities into actual abilities. Acknowledging the ways that socialization has the potential both to foster and to impede one's development of the skills needed for autonomy competency, Meyers notes how the particular values of one's culture inevitably form one's sense of self, as well as which goods, values, and goals will be affirmed and pursued. One's particular enculturation shapes one's motivations and aspirations, encouraging and reinforcing the development of some qualities and skills rather than others. According to Meyers, the sole criterion for oppressive socialization is its failure to cultivate and reinforce the skills of self-discovery, self-definition, and self-direction necessary for an autonomous life. Persons in oppressive contexts may be able to choose autonomously what they really want in circumscribed instances but will likely have difficulty forming an autonomous life plan out of overarching values and goals.

As an example of oppressive socialization, Meyers draws on social scientific research to demonstrate how feminine socialization impedes the development of autonomy skills to a greater degree than masculine socialization. She argues that feminine socialization does not encourage cultivating the skills needed for self-definition and self-direction to the degree that masculine socialization does. Instead, females are socialized to be altruistic and put others' welfare above their own desires and personal development. They also define themselves according to the judgments of others to a greater extent than their male peers. Such socialization narrows their perception of the range of values, goals, and possibilities they can affirm for themselves, distorting their perceptions of themselves and who they can become. Ultimately, an oppressive environment can hinder women from developing an adequate degree of autonomy competency to distinguish their authentic desires from apparent desires, and to achieve an authentic, integrated self.[69]

Because oppressive socialization presents serious obstacles to developing personal autonomy, Meyers argues that justice requires society to be committed to renouncing and eliminating cultural beliefs and values that fuel oppressive socialization practices: "Socializing some people to be minimally autonomous inflicts a serious injury on them."[70] For Meyers, achieving social justice requires creating social conditions that enable all persons to acquire a complex set of skills necessary for autonomy. Why is this the case? First, she argues that an adequate degree of autonomy competency forms the basis for self-respect, and self-respect, in turn, is essential to motivate persons to pursue social and economic opportunities. Meyers defines self-respect as believing in one's inherent worth and dignity as a person and having a favorable attitude toward oneself. Experiencing a sense of personal integration and control over the course of one's life (made possible by autonomy competency) fosters a positive self-concept and self-respect, whereas feeling insecure and conflicted about one's identity and being unable to act in accordance with one's values and goals reinforces a negative self-concept. Such lack of self-efficacy and lack of integration makes a person more vulnerable to personal dissatisfaction and negative self-esteem that erodes self-respect. This creates a vicious cycle, distorting an individual's perceptions of her potentialities and undermining her motivation to pursue opportunities that correspond to her interests. Second, a just society must foster autonomy skills, because minimally autonomous persons lack the skills needed to discern their real desires from heteronomous desires that are accepted unquestioningly from social conventions. If this is the case, they obviously are not in a position to decide which opportunities are consonant with their values, their goals, and their visions of who they are striving to become.

Evaluating Meyers's Autonomous Self in the Context of Trauma

In the context of issues raised by trauma theory, Meyers's account of autonomy successfully addresses the pervasive effects of trauma on the self, and it illuminates ways trauma survivors can increase their degree of autonomy—a crucial feature in the process of recovery and healing. After exploring the strengths of her theory, I will nonetheless indicate why her procedural account of autonomy is insufficient by itself to construct a theological understanding of freedom.

The first advantage of Meyers's conception of a relational self in process, evolving through interactions with others, is that it helps make intelligible the overarching trajectory of traumatization and the fragmentation of self that results from incestuous abuse. Since a coherent self-concept and the exercise of autonomy are viewed by Meyers as accomplishments resulting from the development of complex skills (not as a priori characteristics), incest victims' experiences of severe self-fragmentation make sense within Meyers's philosophical framework. In the case of incest, Meyers would recognize that a child's care providers have not only failed to foster her autonomy skills but also have violated the most basic capacities that make possible her emerging self. Repudiating the idea that free will is a given resulting from reason,[71] it is not surprising—according to Meyers's theory—that trauma victims appear to be unable to transcend the negative effects of traumatization or "pull themselves up by their bootstraps." In other words, Meyers's account of the relational self makes clear that traumatic events and posttraumatic sequelae are not merely external threats to freedom and the self; they are insidiously and pervasively internalized in the very formation of the self.

Furthermore, Meyers's philosophical framework provides insight into the ways that generally oppressive dimensions of female socialization magnify the negative effects of incestuous abuse. As if sexual abuse were not enough to prevent a person from forming a coherent sense of self and the ability to act freely, there are forms of socialization that shape interpretations of sexual abuse, further conspiring to undermine positive development. The complex interplay between specific traumatic events and patterns of socialization demonstrate why incest victims are "sitting ducks" for further victimization and other forms of traumatic reenactment. This also allows us to see how socialization has the potential both to exacerbate posttraumatic stress and foster recovery. Meyers's notion of a relational self shows why supportive relationships are so essential in the process of recovery. These are required for the development of communication and interpersonal skills that are intrinsic to achieving autonomy competency. Using intersubjective skills, trauma survivors can dialogue with others and receive feedback on how to foster a positive self-concept; reflect critically on their desires, values, and goals; imagine new constructive possibilities for their future; and resist harmful social pressures as they act in ways consonant with their emerging life plan.

Meyers's account of autonomy provides a clear, practical framework for helping trauma victims understand how to develop the skills needed to achieve a meaningful sense of self-determination. This view of autonomy formation embraces the concept of formulating a life plan. It requires trauma survivors to reflect on their values, goals, and priorities. By emphasizing that autonomy is achieved in varying degrees, it offers concrete guidelines for developing the skills of self-inquiry, self-definition (discerning personal standards), and self-direction (acting in accordance with one's life plan). It also challenges the false dichotomy in societal interpretations of trauma victims, seeing them as either helpless victims (a condescending attitude that further disempowers them) or as free agents responsible for their own suffering (an attitude that results in blaming the victim). Each of these attitudes, left unchallenged, can prevent the development of autonomy skills and the formation of a positive sense of self.

Finally, besides applying her autonomy model on an individualistic level, Meyers helps to raise societal consciousness about the relation between achieving justice and ensuring conditions needed to cultivate autonomy. In regard to the political dimensions of sexual abuse and its effects on autonomy, Meyers could argue that justice requires bold preventive steps to reduce the incidence of sexual abuse present in society. In addition to advocacy for relevant legislation and social programs, Meyers's perspective could lead to a critique of the cultural beliefs and socialization practices that fuel sexual exploitation of children and women.

While Meyers's theory of autonomy helps us to understand better the dynamics of traumatization and the conditions for recovery, her view that procedural criteria alone can adequately distinguish autonomous desires from heteronomous ones and ensure genuine autonomy fails to be convincing. According to Meyers, as long as an individual has reasonable skills for self-inquiry, good discernment of personal standards and ideals, and appropriate action in accordance with those standards, she can distinguish "real" autonomous desires from heteronomous desires instilled by socialization. In this way, persons can be confident that they are leading an autonomous life. Note that the actual content of one's desires and values is not relevant for evaluating autonomy. Meyers argues that, out of respect for the diversity and uniqueness of persons, one cannot expect that autonomous persons will share substantive goods, let alone particular values or goals.

Unfortunately, it is doubtful that Meyers's procedural account is sufficient to distinguish autonomous desires from the "unhealthy" desires that arise from traumatic injuries or unjust socialization. Meyers herself notes that her interest in developing an account of autonomy was sparked by the following problem: "If women's professed desires are products of their inferior position, should we give credence to those desires? If so, we seem to be capitulating to institutionalize injustice by gratifying warped desires."[72] Her constructive response promises procedural criteria that identify which desires are autonomous, hence worthy of respect, and which are warped and for that reason not to be publicly legitimated. To evaluate whether procedural criteria are sufficient, consider the case of an incest survivor named Lauren who is trying to decide whether to act out sadomasochistic desires and fantasies.[73] While Lauren adequately exercises all the skills (introspective, communication, memory, imaginative, analytic, volitional, and interpersonal) necessary for an autonomous agent, such desires and fantasies continue to dominate her thoughts. Within Meyers's account of autonomy, Lauren may view the ratification of such desires as truly autonomous. After all, there are no substantive criteria in Meyers's theory of autonomy that rule out the possibility that sadomasochistic fantasies can be "authentic" desires. Nothing in her theory challenges "authenticity" if desires are merely in harmony with one another.

According to Meyers, Lauren's utilization of her autonomy competency would prevent her from being "completely abandoned" to her enculturation and enable her to formulate "her own" criteria about what is good and fulfilling in her life.[74] However, are we confident that Lauren's autonomy skills equip her with these abilities? More likely, her sexual desires to act sadomasochistically are desires she internalized throughout her abusive relationship with her father. If she were to act on these desires, she would then be reenacting traumatic dynamics from her past abuse and remain trapped within the cycle of victimization. Due to this likelihood, we have every reason to suspect that such desires are not autonomous and authentic. It begins to look as if a person's desires and actions can qualify as autonomous under Meyers's procedural account and yet be nothing more than an untroubled internalization of cultural norms or abusive dynamics in past relationships.

Meyers's endorsement of a solely procedural account of autonomy is problematic to the degree that it underestimates the extent to which desires and values can be internalized and appropriated (consciously and unconsciously) prior to the gradual mastery of autonomous skills. It seems quite likely that one can easily internalize "warped" (that is, self-destructive) desires resulting from oppressive socialization,[75] subsequently employ all of the skills involved in autonomy competency to reflect on such desires, and still embrace them as "one's own." For this overarching reason, I find Meyers's procedural account of autonomy insufficient, especially for persons like incest survivors who are seeking to discern the extent to which they are acting autonomously, and who must guard against a propensity toward revictimization and self-destructiveness.[76]

Thus, while I agree with Meyers that developing autonomy skills is a necessary condition for a person to act freely and achieve an authentic sense of self, substantive criteria are also needed for an adequate philosophical conception of autonomy. At the very least, substantive values like self-respect and self-worth ought to be included to determine genuine autonomy. Such values show clearly why Lauren's masochistic desires, which ultimately demean her, cannot be considered autonomous.

The significance of substantive criteria when discerning what constitutes an authentic self and freedom intensifies if one affirms a theological framework. The Christian tradition, drawing on resources not acknowledged by philosophy, offers a thicker, normatively richer description of the "authentic" self and freedom than Meyers's secular theory of autonomy. Since my objective in this book is to articulate a revised theology of freedom and grace, it is helpful to identify points of contrast between Meyers's and Christian theology's criteria for authenticity. As noted, Meyers's authentic self emerges from the exercise of autonomy competency. The characteristics of this self are entirely open-ended and depend on the preferences of the individual. Authenticity and autonomy seem, finally, to consist only in the harmony or coherence of one's desires, whatever these might be. In contrast, within a theological framework that affirms a God who creates persons out of love for the purpose of loving others and sharing in divine being, the "authentic self" is not open-ended but is measurable in terms of God's intentions for creation. Similarly, a Christian concept of freedom is more radical than Meyers's idea that autonomy consists simply of accordance with what one really wants. For instance, if I exercise my repertoire of autonomy skills flawlessly and only care about my family members and becoming wealthy, I would be considered successfully autonomous according to Meyers's procedural account, since my desires cohere. Within the framework of the Christian tradition, however, I would be interpreted as a selfish individual who has turned away from realizing my freedom to grow in love for God and neighbor. As noted, theological freedom is not a choice between one object and another; it is not a choice concerning which personality characteristics one wishes to integrate into one's authentic self. Theological freedom involves ultimate self-disposal whereby one accepts or rejects communion with God. Because the task of this book is to articulate a theology of freedom that is responsive to trauma survivors' experiences, there is good reason not to rely solely on Meyers's procedural criteria for an account of freedom; substantive criteria are also essential when discerning what constitutes an authentic self and freedom in a theological framework.

Conclusion

Despite limitations in Butler's and Meyers's accounts of selfhood and agency, I have identified positive and useful insights that resonate with the experiences of trauma victims. Both Butler and Meyers argue that agency cannot be presumed as a "given" ontological attribute, which clarifies why trauma victims become so ensnared in the dynamics of traumatization. Learning how social discourses exacerbate the effects of incestuous abuse and contribute to traumatization can aid trauma survivors in their recovery. Meyers's procedural account of autonomy can be especially useful for trauma survivors, shedding light on how to develop skills needed for acting freely and assuming responsibility for one's life. Such insights, I argue, are crucial when constructing a revised theology of freedom that satisfactorily attends to the reality of severely traumatized persons. In the next chapter, then, I analyze how feminist theory and the experiences of trauma survivors challenge the credibility of Rahner's theology, and then seek to respond to this challenge.

5

Response to the Challenge

Rahner's Theology Revisited

The aim of this chapter is to revisit Rahner's theology of freedom in light of challenges raised by extreme loss of freedom experienced as a result of severe trauma, particularly the sort explored in chapter 3. At times, Rahner's understanding of the self, freedom, and grace appears almost irrelevant to the concrete situations of incest victims. This is because his well-known writings on grace and freedom do not explicitly acknowledge the severe extent to which interpersonal harm can damage our freedom to receive and respond to God's grace. The result, unfortunately, is a loss of potential for Rahner's theology to foster healing and recovery for trauma victims. Most significantly, if incest victims' experiences suggest the possibility that severe interpersonal harm may crush an individual's ability to realize freedom and effect a fundamental option, God's grace by itself appears unable to guarantee human freedom. Rahner's fundamental position on grace and freedom is thus called into question.

There are, however, a number of insightful passages within Rahner's lesser known writings that address some of these issues. My objective is to draw on these insights, along with contributions from feminist and trauma theory, to advance a revised Rahnerian account of the human self, freedom, and grace. The revised account preserves key elements of Rahner's ideas on grace and freedom and also takes seriously the realities of trauma victims.

Trauma's Challenge to Rahner's Conception of the Self and Freedom

In his most well-known writings, Rahner's theological anthropology appears to conflict fundamentally with important conceptions of the self and human freedom as they emerge in feminist and trauma theory. Rahner depicts persons as endowed with a self-consciousness that makes possible the capacity to transcend who they presently are as they actualize their potentialities and grow into the fullness of who they are meant to be. For Rahner, subjectivity includes capacities for self-awareness, self-reflection, and self-transcendence. These are all dependent on the possession of reason. According to Rahner, the only persons whose subjectivity and freedom (transcendental and categorical) are in doubt are those who lack reason: the mentally handicapped, children who die before the age of reason, and the unborn.[1] He brackets these as exceptions and confines his account of freedom to persons who possess rationality and hence subjectivity. Besides requiring reason to attain subjectivity, Rahner acknowledges that, as spirits-in-the-world, persons are dependent on others and the world in the sense that they must interact with other finite beings to become aware of themselves as knowing subjects capable of distinguishing between finitude and the horizon of infinite being. The human self therefore relies on interactions with other persons to experience transcendence and self-actualization. Since Rahner does not specify whether persons require a certain kind of interaction (supportive rather than abusive and traumatic), the reader is left with the impression that any kind of interpersonal interaction is sufficient to realize subjectivity.

In contrast, feminist philosophers like Diana Meyers argue that self-knowledge, self-reflection, and self-transcendence depend on more than reason and mere interaction with one's environment. The experiences of incest victims, too, strongly suggest that developing sufficient degrees of these capabilities is contingent on the absence of overwhelming stress and oppressive socialization, as well as the presence of supportive relationships. One's capacity for self-consciousness and transcendence is usually not entirely destroyed by bodily violations, abusive relationships, and oppression. However, the desire to know more, grow, explore, place everything into question, and be open to further possibilities is deeply influenced by one's material and social conditions. Chronic interpersonal harm can dramatically limit and constrict an individual's horizons and her anticipation of future possibilities. In other words, trauma and other interpersonal harms like oppressive socialization (as described by Butler and Meyers) can gravely diminish the degree to which one experiences the varying forms of self-transcendence and subjectivity that, according to Rahner, are needed for genuinely free actions.

Incest and other trauma victims undoubtedly possess reason in the sense understood by Rahner. But if an adequate degree of subjectivity, with its capacity for self-transcendence, does not follow simply from rationality, and if individuals require supportive human relationships to develop these capacities, then Rahner's stance that transcendental and categorical freedom are constitutive of subjectivity is also challenged. Rahner believes that "man cannot be anything but free once he comes to the awareness of self," and he is confident that reason gives persons the ability to reflect on the way in which external factors have determined who they have become.[2] As noted in chapter 2, in light of such self-reflection, persons have options regarding how they will respond and change:

> The subject . . . is challenged to say something and to do something with man's absolute dependence and self-alienation and determination, challenged to take a position on it by either cursing it or accepting it. . . . So even when a person would abandon himself into the hands of empirical anthropologies, he still remains in his own hands. He does not escape from his freedom, and the only question can be how he interprets himself, and freely interprets himself.[3]

While this self-reflection is possible to some extent for incest victims, their overall skills for self-reflection can be radically compromised even though they still possess reason. As we have seen, the fragmentation of the self that consequently diminishes self-awareness, self-coherency, self-continuity, and self-worth vastly impedes the capacity for self-understanding and agency. Suffering from trauma-related mental and physical disorders like depression, anxiety, hyperarousal, emotional numbing, autonomic arousal, eating disorders, and suicidal ideation inhibits the capacity for self-reflection and effective agency. Compulsively reenacting the trauma throughout one's life further calls into question the extent to which trauma, along with its posttraumatic sequelae, impedes incest victims' capacity for free self-determining actions. Thus, incest victims' experiences and feminist insights concerning the pervasive extent to which the self can be fragmented by oppressive discourses indicate that Rahner underestimates the extent to which interpersonal harm can thwart the development of adequate subjectivity and freedom. Reason simply cannot be the only criterion to evaluate a person's attainment of subjectivity, freedom, and responsibility.

Above all, such fragmentation of the self and compromised categorical freedom challenge Rahner's confidence that persons endowed with reason have sufficient freedom for ultimate self-disposal. Of course, Rahner does acknowledge that some actions in a person's life are more of the nature of imposed necessity than freedom and thus do not influence one's fundamental option. Incest victims' self-destructive actions may fall into this category of necessity and thus would not influence their transcendental response to God's self-offer. However, while acknowledging that some actions may fall into the category of imposed necessity, Rahner presumes that persons commit enough sufficiently free actions to realize a "yes" or "no" to God throughout their lifetimes. It is precisely this presumption that is called into question by some incest victims' lives: confronted with innumerable stories of severely abused girls who run away from home only to be victimized repeatedly and caught in a never-ending cycle of traumatization, and who, on account of prostitution, drug abuse, AIDS, murder, and so on, suffer premature death, is it credible to take for granted that everyone commits enough sufficiently free actions to realize a "yes" to God?[4] Could it be that the damage these incest victims and other trauma victims sustain means that their freedom to effect a fundamental option may not be realized in their temporal existence? If so, what does this say about a theology of freedom that makes a fundamental option the center of what it means to be human?

Trauma's Challenge to Rahner's Account of Grace

If the experiences of incest victims call into question Rahner's account of freedom, they also challenge his understanding of the workings of God's grace in at least three fundamental ways. First, the extreme degree of suffering experienced by incest victims leads us to question specifically the power and efficacy of God's grace. We may wonder why we do not see more "evidence" of the healing quality of God's grace in the lives of persons who experience severe threats to their bodily and psychological integrity. Rahner's claim that God's self-communication brings about ontological, transformative changes in human consciousness that enable our freedom to respond to God's grace can appear incredible when confronted with the realities of many incest victims who are ensnared in the cycle of traumatization and may resort to suicide as the only escape from their unbearable suffering.

As we have seen, Rahner frequently claims that persons are given sufficient grace to receive and respond to divine grace.[5] God's overflowing grace enables a person to open herself to God's love, to know God as a "hidden closeness, a forgiving intimacy, a real home... as a love which shares itself, something familiar which he can approach and turn to from the estrangement of his own perilous and empty life."[6] Yet opening oneself to God in the way that Rahner describes presupposes an ability to experience trust in another—the very sort of practical achievement that can be seriously damaged by chronic interpersonal harm. When we take seriously many incest victims' despair at experiencing only silence, distance, betrayal, and judgment from God, it does not seem credible to assume at the outset that divine grace heals victims' seriously impaired capacity to trust and enables them to open themselves to God's love.

Furthermore, reflecting on the severe extent to which one's self and agency can be shattered by incestuous abuse and other traumas, God's grace does not appear to protect sufficiently one's core sense of self and freedom from the destructive effects of interpersonal sin and evil. In instances when incest survivors are tragically subject to abusive relationships rather than supportive ones, God's grace does not seem to compensate for the absence of loving, interpersonal relationships and its destructive effects; in other words, grace does not appear to enable many persons to transcend the posttraumatic effects of abuse, specifically to overcome their compulsion to reenact the trauma and recover on their own. Rahner's construal of grace as providing a sufficient condition to enable human freedom is thus seriously called into question. This challenge undoubtedly raises the question of human evil and its potential power to limit the efficacy of God's grace. The experience of severely traumatized persons compels us to pose the question: does human evil have the power to damage our ability to respond to God's grace, thereby limiting God's ability to communicate grace effectively to all persons?

Second, incest victims' experiences press us to inquire more deeply how, according to Rahner, God mediates divine grace to all persons. In his most well-known articles on grace and freedom, Rahner does not typically focus on how God mediates grace; instead, he seems content simply to assert that God somehow provides the graced condition to enable our freedom to effect a fundamental option. Rahner frequently describes God's self-offer to every person as effecting ontological, transformative changes in human consciousness that make possible our freedom for ultimate self-disposal. As noted in chapter 2, these transformative effects, called created gifts of grace, elevate and heal human nature, enabling each individual to accept God's self-offer. Reading these passages, the reader can easily be led to imagine that, despite horrendous evils, God's grace mysteriously provides the graced condition to enable each person's free choice to love God, self, and others. Many incest victims' extreme loss of adequate subjectivity and freedom, however, presses us to inquire how exactly (if at all) this graced condition is mediated.

Rahner argues that the transcendental offer of God's self-communication is necessarily mediated categorically through the historical life of each person and the history of humankind. While the mediation of God's self-communication attains its greatest clarity through Christ and subsequently through the Church, Rahner claims that our experience of God and divine grace is historically mediated by any categorical event in which a subject experiences subjectivity and freedom: humans' "supernaturally elevated transcendentality is . . . mediated to itself by *any and every categorical reality* in which and through which the subject becomes present to itself."[7] Such mediation of God's self-communication, then, can take place "everywhere" in our encounters with the world and especially with other people.[8]

The experiences of trauma victims, however, indicate that it is insufficient for Rahner to remain at this level of generality. Not just any kind of interaction with the world and others is sufficient to mediate God's self-offer along with the graced condition to respond. Experiences of both traumatization and recovery strongly suggest that supportive relationships with others are a primary way in which God's self-communication and the graced condition to accept this offer are categorically mediated to persons. If it actually is the case that supportive relationships are necessary to mediate the transcendental divine self-offer along with sufficient grace for human freedom, we return to questions about the power and efficacy of God's grace in instances where persons suffer from chronic abuse and lack of support.

Third, trauma victims' experiences also challenge the adequacy of Rahner's paradigmatic descriptions of experiences of grace. Rahner overwhelmingly emphasizes two themes when describing our encounters with divine grace: (1) moments when the self transcends egoism and selflessly loves God and others, and (2) moments in which one experiences suffering. Consider the following descriptions of persons experiencing grace and positively responding to God's self-offer.

> Have we ever kept quiet, even though we wanted to defend ourselves when we had been unfairly treated? Have we ever forgiven someone even though we got no thanks for it and our silent forgiveness was taken for granted? Have we ever obeyed, not because we had to and because otherwise things would have become unpleasant for us, but simply on account of that mysterious, silent, incomprehensible being we call God and his will? Have we ever sacrificed something without receiving any thanks or recognition for it, and even without a feeling of inner satisfaction? Have we ever been absolutely lonely? . . . Have we ever fulfilled a duty when it seemed that it could be done only with a consuming sense of really betraying and obliterating oneself, when it could apparently be done only by doing

> something terribly stupid for which no one would thank us? Have we ever been good to someone who did not show the slightest sign of gratitude or comprehension and when we also were not rewarded by the feeling of having been "selfless," decent, etc.?[9]

> When we have let ourselves go and no longer belong to ourselves, when we have denied ourselves and no longer have the disposing of ourselves, when everything (including ourselves) has moved away from us as if into an infinite distance, then we begin to live in the world of God himself, the world of the God of grace.[10]

> Only if one thus abandons oneself, and lovingly sinks into the other, does one succeed in finding oneself. Otherwise, a person languishes in the prison of his or her own selfishness.[11]

While Rahner does acknowledge in one essay that we can experience God through positive experiences of "surpassing joy" and the experience of "an absolute responsibility, faithfulness or love," he resists drawing on these experiences as paradigmatic.[12] In his article "Reflections on the Experience of Grace," Rahner even questions whether such positive experiences are truly "experiences of the spirit in its proper transcendence."[13]

Rahner's emphases on self-denial and surrender to God as paradigmatic experiences of grace fit perfectly within his central narrative of the human self seeking to overcome egoism and actualize a fundamental option for God. For Rahner's subject who possesses moral agency and a sufficiently developed self, these experiences of transcending self-interest are powerful depictions of grace and free actions of neighbor-love that gradually realize a "yes" to God. Embracing these as defining, paradigmatic moments of grace, however, raises special problems if trauma victims are part of the intended theological audience. Suggesting that incest victims ought to act in such "selfless" ways would likely signal not the "hour of grace" and the presence of "the Holy Spirit who is at work in us" but a dangerous, self-destructive scenario.[14] Obeying, keeping quiet, forgiving perpetrators and other family members who failed to offer protection, and sacrificing personal interests are frequently the very actions abusive families expect from incest victims—selfless actions that perpetuated the chronic sexual abuse when they were children. If incest victims are part of a religious community where these acts are praised as "model" experiences of grace, they will likely be retraumatized by selflessness, feel ashamed in their attempts at self-assertion and self-protection, and be thwarted overall in their process of recovery. Similarly, Rahner's moves to affirm "letting ourselves go," "no longer belonging to our selves," and denying and abandoning ourselves provide eerie echoes of the dissociative experiences that increase self-fragmentation. Also likely to promote self-destructive behavior and revictimization from others is the advice to fulfill a duty that may betray and obliterate the self, be good to those who are not grateful, and "lovingly sink into another."

Relating Rahner's dominant narrative to incest victims' reality is fraught with difficulty. In the first place, ego transcendence and neighbor-love do not accurately characterize their main struggles in life. After all, the dominant theme in many trauma victims' lives appears to be the daily struggle to survive at all, both psychologically and physically.[15] The effort to cope with PTSD and other long-term effects of incestuous abuse leaves many incest victims with little energy and attention to pursue higher aims of self-realization. Rather than striving to overcome self-interest to serve the welfare of others, incest victims struggle to attain more basic interpersonal skills: simply tolerating the physical touch of another, feeling a sense of connectedness with others, trusting and experiencing empathy, and avoiding abusive relations that reenact past trauma. They are, as we have seen, often caught in compulsive patterns of reenacting trauma by harming themselves and others, being revictimized in subsequent relationships, and failing to protect others, including their children, from being harmed. They experience feeling "dead" inside and an inability to empathize.

The upshot is that accepting Rahner's account of God's grace,[16] at this stage of our analysis, appears to commit us to the belief that divine grace must *somehow*, even in light of powerful evidence to the contrary, enable incest victims' freedom to act selflessly in their love for God and neighbor. And following the logical implications of this position, we are likely to view incest victims as ultimately culpable for any inability to undertake loving actions toward themselves, others, and God. Any failure here must amount to acquiescence to the temptation of sin pervading each person's life. Consequently, there is no significant distinction between (1) a trauma victim struggling to love others and God and (2) Rahner's untraumatized self who, though burdened by the possibility of sin as a permanent existential, finds free decisions to love selflessly and transcend egoism difficult but possible.

Response to the Challenge

Sometimes theologians in the face of such challenges have appealed simply to mystery: it is not for our limited understanding to fathom the ways God's grace sufficiently enables each person's freedom to love God and neighbor. We simply ought to be confident that grace somehow makes such freedom possible. In the situation we are addressing, however, an appeal to mystery is theologically and pastorally problematic, for it is likely to increase incest victims' shame and alienation and/or lead others to blame victims. Any belief that God somehow provides the graced condition to enable our freedom to love God and others may also exacerbate incest and other trauma victims' feelings of abandonment by God. Incest victims may be plagued by the following kind of question: "If God enables our freedom by offering grace, why doesn't God bestow more grace upon me to heal and enable me to attain a minimal level of functioning so I can survive and love others?" Such beliefs and questions are likely to fuel feelings of God's absence and unavailability that already plague many incest victims.

Rahner's own commitment to take human experience seriously suggests that a simple appeal to mystery would be neither his theological escape nor his ultimate pastoral response. If confronted with contemporary trauma studies, Rahner probably would have taken steps to qualify his theology to avoid the danger of blaming trauma victims for their compulsive traumatic reenactments. What grounds this expectation? First, Rahner consistently demonstrates a methodological commitment to take human experience into account when formulating theological doctrines; his theological method makes it highly unlikely that he would have dismissed the collective experiences of incest and other trauma victims. Second, Rahner argues that theology must take into account the contemporary insights of the sciences and allow itself to be conditioned by them.[17] Third, there are within Rahner's writings at least two places where he appears to waver from his frequent claim that human receptivity and responsiveness to grace is not entirely vulnerable to earthly contingencies.

Precisely these passages within Rahner's own texts may be used to construct a more adequate Rahnerian account of freedom and grace, one that takes seriously incest victims' experiences of both traumatization and recovery. Such an account must incorporate two central claims consistent with trauma and feminist theory. First, there is a sober *possibility* that interpersonal harm can severely, and perhaps entirely, impair one's freedom to effect a fundamental option. Such a claim attends explicitly to the significant degree to which bodily violations and interpersonal harm affect one's sense of self, freedom, relationality, and ability to respond to God's grace. Second, a revised account of freedom and grace acknowledging this possibility must also shed light on the workings of God's grace within the lives of incest survivors. Theological reflection on the experiences of trauma survivors' process of recovery, I argue, strongly suggests that a primary way God seeks to communicate grace is indirectly through loving, interpersonal relations. While Rahner never denies the idea that God mediates grace through supportive relationships, this particular idea is insufficiently developed in his most well-known writings on grace. To develop further the theological implications of this idea, I therefore find it important to draw on some of Rahner's reflections about grace in his more pastoral writings.

Confronting the Possibility of Interpersonal Harm Destroying Freedom

Even to consider the possibility that interpersonal harm has the power to incapacitate a person's freedom for ultimate self-disposal may appear deeply antithetical to Christian faith and hope in the power of God's grace. It suggests that human moral evil has the potential to triumph over the efficacy of God's grace at definitive moments in a person's life. One might argue that coherency with the Christian tradition leaves no other option than embracing the belief that God somehow mysteriously enables transcendental freedom even in cases where one's categorical freedom appears nonexistent.[18] Due to the effects of interpersonal harm, an incest victim's "yes" to God must be facilitated by grace at a level completely undetectable in experience. Or perhaps an incest victim's "yes" to God is manifest in her daily acts of resistance, in her ability to have survived for as long as she has. Either of these possibilities could suffice for a fundamental option.

No doubt Christians are called to hope that God does somehow enable all persons to effect a fundamental option, despite the constraints brought about by interpersonal harm. However, we must be wary of assuming that the outcomes of this hope are always fulfilled in victory. There is a difference between embracing such hope and presuming that it corresponds to the reality of all persons' lives. Indeed, there are potential theological problems with completely dismissing the prospect that a person can destroy another's capacity to actualize a "yes" to God. First, insisting that a "yes" to God can occur in a way that is completely undetectable and unrelated to explicit love of neighbor fundamentally conflicts with Rahner's insistence that transcendental and categorical freedom are not two forms of freedom but "two moments which form the single unity of freedom."[19] Moreover, Rahner is clear that categorical acts realizing a "yes" to God amount to more than being a "decent" person who does not harm others; rather, love of God and neighbor makes a "total demand on man out of the situation of his 'hour,' of his call."[20]

Second, we must be cautious of any urges to dismiss the prospect of profound harm, because this stance might actually be functioning to buttress our tendency to deny and minimize the extent to which evil can harm persons.[21] Claiming that interpersonal harm cannot definitively incapacitate a response to God's self-offer may avert our eyes to the power of evil, allowing us to cling to a false sense of protection at the expense of neglecting the suffering and needs of those most harmed. According to Rahner, denying the reality of evil is deeply opposed to authentic Christian faith:

> The comprehensive task of a Christian . . . is the acceptance of human existence as such as opposed to a final protest against it. But this means that a Christian sees reality as it is. Christianity obliges him . . . to see this existence as dark and bitter and hard, and as an unfathomable and radical risk.[22]

Ultimately, then, the most prudent theological position is to emphasize that the mystery of God's grace and human freedom prevents us from affirming or denying with certainty that one's transcendental freedom can be destroyed by interpersonal harm. Our crucial responsibility simply begins by acknowledging certain things we can confidently know from trauma victims' experiences: human sin against one's neighbor can gravely, and perhaps entirely, incapacitate that person's freedom to actualize a "yes" to God's self-offer in the fullness God intends. The possibility that freedom may be destroyed by others' sin is of key significance for Rahner, insofar as God creates each person to be able to grow in love for God and neighbor and actualize a "yes" to God's self-offer. We will examine further the theological implications of acknowledging this possibility of profound harm in what follows.

A Rahnerian Accommodation of Profound Harm

While there may be compelling reasons to consider profound harm—the destruction of one's ability to effect a fundamental option—as a possibility, one might wonder whether we do not thereby definitively depart from a Rahnerian understanding of human freedom and God's grace. While Rahner acknowledges that persons influence the sphere and possibilities of their neighbors' freedom, he frequently claims that persons endowed with reason have the inescapable task of saying yes or no to God's self-offer. These often-repeated claims suggest that the concept of profound harm fundamentally contradicts Rahner's view. Two of his later writings, however, waver from this adamant position and are actually in tension with it; indeed, Rahner is seen grappling with the possibility that exceptional cases may exist in which persons have been incapacitated from effecting a fundamental option. For instance, after defending the religious idea of a fundamental option in his 1976 *Meditations on Freedom and the Spirit*, Rahner feels compelled to introduce the following caveat.

> The idea that man, as a Christian or as the philosophical subject of freedom, is still free, even when he is born in chains, is extremely dubious and may be fundamentally wrong. This is clear from *the fact that* one man can deprive another man by murder (of his biological or psychological reality as a human being) of the possibility of freedom, *even in the theological sense.*[23]

Such a statement suggests that Rahner may have become receptive later in his life to the idea that, in extreme instances, a person (such as an incest perpetrator) has the power to deprive another of his or her "psychological reality as a human being" and incapacitate him or her from realizing sufficient freedom to effect a fundamental option. Similarly, in his article "Christian Dying," originally published in 1978, Rahner briefly mentions the possibility that some adults may actually die before realizing sufficient freedom to say yes or no to God:

> Every human being and Christian has to admit that in his own life he must allow concretely for such an absolute and definitive history of freedom and can never discard the burden of such a responsibility, that he must presume such a history of freedom in every other human being when he encounters rational life in freedom in the course of his secular experience. But . . . it can be said that in the last resort we do not know how or whether this doctrine of the always unique history of freedom passing through death into finality is to be applied to those who die *before* the moment at which, on the basis of ordinary experience, we would be inclined to ascribe to them an actual decision of freedom in the radical sense; nor do we know whether in fact everyone who is "adult" in the sense generally understood really makes *that* decision of freedom. . . . From the Christian standpoint, all that we can really say must be about the "normal case" of human and Christian life, we must take this seriously on each occasion for ourselves, read official teachings of the Church which seem to go beyond this normal case more or less as broad, general statements, not intended in the last resort to express anything purely and simply about marginal, if very numerous, cases; for the rest, we must admit an ignorance which in the last resort is obvious from the nature of the case.[24]

In this passage, Rahner claims that there is no way for individuals or the Church to know whether all adults "in the sense generally understood" effect a fundamental option. Marginal cases, he states, may even be numerous. How are we to interpret this passage and its implications for his understanding of human freedom and God's grace? Prior to "Christian Dying," Rahner observed that the only persons whose freedom to effect a fundamental option is questionable are those who lack reason.[25] Furthermore, Rahner claimed that an individual's sphere of freedom can change the possibilities of others' sphere of freedom but not the actual freedom for self-disposal: "True, I do not change their freedom, but the sphere in which their freedom is realized, hence this affects the possibilities of their subjective freedom."[26] Raising the prospect of exceptions suggests that Rahner became more sympathetic later in his life to the possibility that interpersonal harms can severely disable the human capacity to effect a fundamental option.

Interestingly, however, Rahner does not account for this departure from his earlier stance, expressed in articles in *Theological Investigations* and *Foundations*, that persons endowed with reason inevitably face the task of effecting a fundamental option. He also does not comment on whether the likelihood of exceptional cases calls into question his basic claim that God provides sufficient grace to enable a response to the divine self-offer.

Those who wish to dismiss the possibility of profound harm to another's freedom or who wish to dismiss Rahner's theology as unable to deal with such harm might argue that the foregoing passages are anomalous insofar as they fundamentally contradict and undermine Rahner's repeated insistence that rational persons cannot avoid effecting a fundamental option. They might argue that Rahner does not consistently acknowledge the idea of possible exceptions in his later writings, and actually continues to affirm that all rational persons cannot avoid the inescapable task of deciding for or against God. For instance, in his 1983 work *The Love of Jesus and the Love of Neighbor*, he claims,

> Christianity is convinced (and here we prescind from the question of infants dying before the age of reason, and other cases generally subsumable under this one, since, when all is said and done, we really know nothing about them, nor need we know anything about them for our purposes here) that, in each one of this anonymous crowd, to whom we ourselves of course belong, the unfathomable coming to pass of such love does take place [positively effecting a fundamental option], or else such a human being is lost entirely through his or her own fault.[27]

Furthermore, my critics may argue that Rahner's anomalous passages acknowledging the prospect of profound harm threatens his entire theology of freedom and his account of God's very purpose for creating persons. As noted, Rahner argues that one should not think that persons who appear to have few material opportunities for realizing their freedom are prevented from doing so, since it would be a "strange arrangement of life by God, if in most cases of this free spiritual creature—which after all is called to realize its being freely—this realization did not come to its proper fulfillment."[28] Granting the possibility that some may avoid this fundamental decision in their lives undermines Rahner's depiction of our personal relation to God as a genuine "dialectical history of salvation between God and man."[29] Rahner has said that salvation "not achieved in freedom cannot be salvation."[30] Thus, a God who creates persons for a purpose they cannot fulfill is impotent, indifferent, or cruel. Such a conception of God is obviously antithetical to Rahner's understanding of God as Holy Mystery, graciously offering Godself to each person.

Finally, critics may argue that Rahner's suggestion that some adults may die before effecting a fundamental option undermines his entire account of grace. How are we to understand Rahner's earlier claim that God as Giver offers Godself as Gift and also provides the condition that enables persons to say yes to God? In regard to these marginal cases of persons who may die before effecting a fundamental option, God appears to be withholding sufficient grace to particular persons—a possibility that contradicts Rahner's affirmation that grace is universal.

In response to these criticisms directed at Rahner's later passages, I argue that his acknowledgment about the possibility that some may die before effecting a fundamental option does not amount to senseless inconsistency or incoherency; instead, it simply signifies the tensions Rahner is seeking to resolve in his most mature reflections concerning the fundamental option. On the one hand, Rahner has an obvious distaste for the ease with which contemporary persons embrace the determinism espoused by various social scientific views and philosophical theories. A determinism that eschews personal responsibility for one's emerging identity is entirely antithetical to Rahner's theological anthropology. Belief in determinism of this sort would only produce complacency and self-pity, rather than challenge one to grow in one's abilities to love one's neighbor as oneself. This leads Rahner to emphasize the finite limitations of the social sciences and urge persons to recognize and accept the awesome responsibility they have for themselves.[31] Since saying either yes or no to God corresponds to God's will for us, Rahner refers to this task as inescapable and describes the human self as a lonely burden to himself or herself; after all, one can never cast this ultimate decision of who she becomes onto others. In these writings, Rahner is seeking to inculcate in his readers an all-consuming sense of responsibility for actualizing a "yes" to God throughout their lives. This is also Rahner's plausible intent when he emphasizes in *The Love of Jesus and Love of Neighbor* that all adults effect a fundamental option. Since he has already stated in "Christian Dying" that his theological reflections are concerned with the "normal" cases of Christian life, he sees no need to repeat that there may be exceptions.

On the other hand, Rahner's later acknowledgment of the possibility that some persons might die before realizing their fundamental option is actually more consistent with two central tenets of his account of freedom than his prior stance that all persons possessing reason effect a fundamental option. These two tenets are (1) that freedom needs to be realized throughout time and (2) that certain human acts are not sufficiently free and do not reflect our transcendental response to God. Regarding the first tenet, Rahner consistently depicts creaturely freedom as needing to be realized through a temporal process that involves interacting with others: "Creaturely freedom is conditioned by the situation; for it does not simply possess itself but it must first gain itself, and this it can do only in the encounter with other freedom, in the common life in the world."[32] Since one's possibilities to enact freedom can be deeply constrained by others' actions, it is conceivable that a person repeatedly harmed by the sins of others through her life may die before obtaining a sufficient degree of freedom for ultimate self-disposal. Incidentally, this insight that freedom is realized through a temporal process resembles Butler's and Meyers's insistence that agency cannot be presumed as a "given" but occurs throughout time. These feminist thinkers, however, emphasize to a greater extent than Rahner the threats that may completely undermine the realization of freedom. In this respect, they underscore an important insight that is often obscured in Rahner's writings concerning freedom.

In regard to the second tenet, Rahner repeatedly recognizes that, due to human finitude and vulnerability, certain actions are more of the "nature of imposed necessity" than free. Since these acts are not sufficiently free, they do not influence our transcendental response to God. Although it is never possible to objectify transcendental freedom and judge which acts are free or unfree, Rahner does identify certain situations in which it is more likely that loss of freedom occurs. In his article "Liberty of the Sick Theologically Considered," he says that it is possible to lose one's ability to choose and act freely in instances of severe physical or psychological illness:

> It is impossible to maintain that the total and final consummation of liberty on the part of the human subject in the direction of finality—i.e. death as total act of liberty—always takes place in immediate proximity to death in the medical sense. In most cases the doctors will have before them a dying person whose condition in any case makes it difficult to conceive (without arbitrary hypotheses) how he could be capable of any radical personal act in this situation—by

> which I mean an act through which he freely disposes of himself and the ultimate meaning of his life in a thoroughly radical way. Moreover, there is no cogent theological reason for postulating the opposite of what the medical situation would lead us to suppose.[33]

Furthermore, in one of his last interviews, Rahner identifies suicide as a moment in which a person has lost the ability to act freely and be held accountable for his actions: "If he really cannot endure it anymore, that means, if he is no longer capable of making a really free decision about himself because of psychological and physiological circumstances and, in these circumstances, takes his own life, then he falls into the hands of the merciful God."[34] If Rahner is to be consistent with this line of thought, he needs to affirm that, if a person's actions have been constrained by severe interpersonal harm throughout her entire life, it is possible that she has not committed enough sufficiently free actions to determine her transcendental stance for or against God before she dies.

More specifically, then, in response to acknowledging profound harm, Rahner can consistently affirm the possibility that some persons may die before realizing their freedom and still retain his conviction that God has created us to be able to respond freely to God's self-communication by loving God and neighbor. As noted, he acknowledges in several writings that some persons die before attaining reason and effecting a fundamental option, but nonetheless maintains that human freedom is central to the divine plan for creation and salvation. He merely needs to acknowledge explicitly the possibility that God's intent for persons in this life to respond freely to God may be thwarted by evil actions of other persons whenever they severely impede another's capacity to effect a fundamental option.[35] As a testament to his commitment that all persons freely accept God's self-offer, Rahner claims, albeit tentatively, that God must find some way to enable infants (and others who die before effecting a fundamental option) to make a free personal decision for God.[36] He even suggests that purgatory might be viewed "as offering opportunities and scope for a postmortal history of freedom to someone who had been denied such a history in his earthly life."[37]

In regard to the criticism that Rahner's later concession undermines his account of grace, it is true that Rahner frequently depicts God as providing sufficient grace to enable each person's ability to effect a fundamental option, despite earthly contingencies occurring in the person's life. However, other pastoral writings of Rahner that we will examine next suggest a broader social understanding of how God's grace is communicated to persons. This interpersonal understanding of the mediation of grace is, at times, in tension with Rahner's claim that grace sufficiently enables human freedom in this lifetime.

To explore this idea further, let us now seek to arrive at a more adequate understanding of God's grace within the context of traumatization.

Grace as Socially Mediated through Supportive Relationships

In order to begin elucidating an account of how God mediates grace that adequately attends to the reality of trauma victims, we again confront questions about the power and efficacy of God's grace and how God mediates such grace to children and adults traumatized by repeated abuse and violence. I propose that incest survivors' experiences of the recovery process, as well as feminist insights about the social dimensions of the self, suggest strongly that a primary way that God conveys grace is through human nurturing, care, and love. As we have seen, trauma literature consistently finds that the dynamics of traumatization render an individual incapable of transcending the totalizing effects of trauma and its posttraumatic stress symptoms on her own. Intervention from a third party is crucial to break the traumatic cycle created by the dynamics of perpetrator and victim. Social scientific research consistently shows that it is during the process of reconnecting with others and learning how to trust that incest victims begin to heal. Within the context of supportive relations, incest survivors are able to form a more constructive sense of self and develop skills needed to exercise effective agency and act freely. They begin to exert a greater sense of control over their actions and are able to take responsibility for the persons they are becoming. In short, the experiences of incest survivors and other trauma victims testify to persons' dependence on the support and love of others to realize their freedom to relate positively to themselves, others, and God.

These experiences of healing, acquiring a new life-giving identity, and feeling liberated to love freely and be loved are often understood within a theological framework as the workings of grace. Since such experiences occur in the context of interpersonal relations, it appears fruitful to inquire whether it is not actually God's grace at work in these liberating experiences. Trauma survivors' experiences strongly suggest that God may have ordered creation and redemption in such a way that God depends on the cooperation of other persons' free choices to love their neighbors for mediating divine grace.

Rahner's Recognition of Grace as Mediated through Supportive Relationships

While Rahner does not develop this idea of grace being mediated through loving relationships in his well-known articles of grace and freedom, some of Rahner's theological reflections on ecclesiology, the Sacraments, and the Holy Spirit support further development of this idea and express a more social view of how God's grace is communicated to persons. For instance, when considering the Church's purpose, Rahner directly addresses the following issue: if God already communicates grace by offering Godself to each person, why do persons need a tangible sign of Christ in the form of an institutional Church? He argues that each person's transcendental relation to God's self-offer must be mediated historically and socially, and that such mediation is necessary for salvation.[38] God's gracious self-offer is revealed in its fullest manifestation historically through the Incarnation of Jesus Christ. The mediation of God's grace, however, does not end with Christ's death and resurrection but needs continual historical and social mediation; primarily, but by no means exclusively, this occurs through the institution of the Church. For Rahner, "the Church is the presence of saving grace in the world."[39]

Why is there such a need for God's grace to be mediated socially? In these discussions, Rahner argues that, due to humanity's historical and social nature, experience of God can only be mediated through fellowship with others:

> There is no experience of God for pilgrim man on this earth which has not been mediated through an experience of the world. Even the immediacy of man to God as constituted by God's self-bestowal in grace . . . is always mediated through the experience of the world which man finds already about him. . . . This relationship to the world . . . is primarily a relationship to a society, the human Thou.[40]

In this passage, Rahner suggests that God relies on others to mediate grace in the world. Even when he analyzes the mediation of grace through the Sacraments in his more pastoral writings, Rahner acknowledges that the Sacraments are not the sole or necessary means of mediating God's grace. He emphasizes that, since sanctifying grace permeates human existence and is mediated in whatever ways the Holy Spirit wills, the Church depends on all members to use their individual, particular charisms bestowed by the Holy Spirit to advance prospects for human liberation and salvation on earth: "There are the charismatic effects of the Spirit . . . which take root in the Church wherever the Spirit himself desires that."[41] Given his understanding of the Holy Spirit, Rahner explicitly claims that the Church, consisting of both the clergy and laity, is called to manifest God's grace to the world: "Each member of the Church actively shares in building up the Church—conveying grace to individual human beings."[42] Consequently, all members, not merely the institution or the clergy, mediate God's grace to one another: "The bringing to accomplishment of this presence [of God's grace] is the act of all those living in God's grace in the

Church. In some form they make this love present and perceptible in the Church's historical and social embodiment."[43]

Furthermore, in his reflections on receiving God's grace via the Sacraments, Rahner emphasizes the importance of grace being mediated interpersonally: "The Sacramental powers attain their purpose only if the recipients are prepared for them by efficacious graces, and these in most cases are mediated by persons who themselves hold no office."[44] All church members, then, take part in the Church's purpose of being a sign of salvation for all: "Every member in the body of Christ can and must serve as a channel of salvation for all others."[45] Such responsibility to serve as the channel of salvation and mediate God's grace, argues Rahner, is grounded in each Christian's unity with Christ.[46]

A Revised Rahnerian Theology of Freedom and Grace

As we see in the foregoing passages, there are moments in Rahner's writings that affirm the possibility for profound harm and the need for God's grace to be mediated socially. Unfortunately, however, Rahner does not incorporate these insights and their implications into his overall account of freedom and grace. If these two claims—(1) that external threats can severely debilitate one's freedom, and (2) that God mediates grace socially through supportive interpersonal relations—are explicitly integrated within Rahner's theology of freedom and grace, the following features of a revised Rahnerian account of freedom and grace become prominent.

As for the self, there is a clear acknowledgment that merely interacting with others is not adequate for ensuring subjectivity and agency. Drawing especially from feminist insights, we recognize explicitly that the *quality* of relationality matters: some form of supportive relationship is essential for developing an adequate degree of subjectivity. Incorporating the experiences of persons traumatized by physical violence, we also appreciate how bodily violations deeply constitute the formation of the self and gravely impede the development of skills needed for subjectivity. While the self is not reducible to one's body, experiences of embodiment do pervasively shape one's formation of subjectivity. This revised Rahnerian understanding of the self, drawing from Butler's insights about social constructionism and Meyers's analysis of oppressive socialization, underscores how demeaning social discourses and practices exacerbate the effects of bodily violation, further eroding the formation of a constructive self-concept and requisite abilities for subjectivity.

With regard to freedom and self-determination, we can still fully embrace Rahner's central conviction that God creates us with the purpose of being able to accept freely God's offer of self-communication and actualize our "yes" to God. However, taking seriously Butler's and Meyers's insistence that freedom is not an invulnerable, ontological attribute, we recognize that realizing our capacity for freedom is dependent to a significant extent on supportive relations. Appreciating the crucial role played by interpersonal relations in the realization of freedom forces us to confront the possibility that persons who lack supportive relations and are subject to repeated interpersonal violations may be deprived of sufficient opportunity for ultimate self-disposal. Christian communities, by acknowledging that interpersonal harm severely damages not only persons' ability to relate lovingly to themselves and others but also to God, can be better equipped to identify ways the Church can offer support to counteract such harms and foster conditions that help persons realize their freedom. Meyers's theoretical framework for the complex set of skills necessary to ensure autonomous actions can be an invaluable resource when discerning appropriate support.

Furthermore, Rahner recognizes in many of his writings that our freedom to actualize ourselves is intersubjective, in the sense that we need others because loving them enables us to realize our "yes" to God and experience authentic fulfillment. A revised Rahnerian understanding of freedom, informed by feminist and trauma theory, equally emphasizes that freedom is also intersubjective in the sense that experiences of *being* loved are crucial for realizing our freedom to become the persons God created us to be.[47] Acknowledging that our ability to act freely and determine who we want to be depends on parents and caregivers carries many implications. The quality of parenting and mentoring becomes more theologically significant than is generally acknowledged, and taking steps to educate parents about how best to foster freedom and a positive relationship with one's self and God becomes more pressing.

Finally, a revised Rahnerian account of freedom that incorporates feminist and trauma theory insights moves beyond Rahner's repeated insistence that our main objective in this life is self-actualization to an explicit emphasis that our main task is to ensure that we and our neighbors have sufficient conditions that enable us to realize our freedom and live out a "yes" to God. No longer able to presume that reason is sufficient to ensure human freedom, we need to investigate how conditions such as abuse, poverty, racism, and other forms of exploitation undercut the concrete realization of human freedom.

As for a revised understanding of the relation between God's grace and human freedom, the insight that supportive relations are necessary for recovery from trauma leads us to highlight that a primary way in which God communicates grace is through the experience of loving, interpersonal relations. If this is true, then we need to confront the possibility that God's attempt to mediate grace can be significantly obstructed by the evil actions of others, when persons have been subject to interpersonal cruelty and utterly deprived of loving, interpersonal relations. God's love is obviously not, for instance, mediated in the experiences of bodily violations, abusive interpersonal relations, and demeaning social dynamics.

Of course, a response could be that interpersonal relations are only one, albeit a primary, component of a person's experience of the world; other experiences in which God's grace may be mediated include the Bible, interacting with nature, animals, literature, social and religious institutions, the arts, and so on. God, according to this view, can still convey sufficient grace and manifest care and concern through other forms of mediation when a person is deprived of all loving, interpersonal relations. While it is credible to believe that God seeks to mediate grace through all dimensions of human existence, we must still acknowledge that incest survivors are indeed exposed to these other forms of interactions and yet continue to suffer from severe fragmentation of self and compromised agency; a significant number of incest survivors still struggle every day merely to survive.

This presses us to question whether these other forms of mediating grace are sufficient in the absence of supportive interpersonal relations to enable the realization of freedom needed to effect a fundamental option. Perhaps God is continuously communicating divine love and mediating grace in all possible ways, but human sin against one's neighbor has the potential power to debilitate the neighbor's capacity to receive and respond to God's grace. A revised Rahnerian account of freedom and God's grace can hope, but cannot presume, that God's grace sufficiently enables one's freedom to effect a fundamental option.

What warrants our hope that persons severely harmed by human evil will be able to receive God's grace and realize their freedom to say yes to God? The good news is that, while human evil has the potential to block God's grace from being effectively communicated to an individual, human love can also become occasions of God's mediating grace. Besides emphasizing that persons encounter grace during experiences of transcendence and selfless love for others, then, it is important to underscore that experiences of grace also occur when we are nurtured, affirmed, and loved by another. The fact that supportive relations are necessary for recovery from severe trauma suggests that God has ordered creation in such a way that God depends significantly on human agency to mediate divine love: whenever persons freely choose to love one another, there exists the potential that God's grace is being mediated and is enabling persons' freedom to realize their "yes" to God.

Accordingly, God entrusts the human community with grave responsibility to foster one another's freedom and be mutual vehicles of God's mediating grace. Therefore, a revised Rahnerian account of freedom and grace affirms that God offers the gift of the divine self to all person and bestows on them the graced potential to accept a destiny of intimate communion with God. No earthly or interpersonal harm can take away this ever-present self-offer and the graced potential to respond to God's self-communication. However, such profound harm can gravely, and perhaps entirely, debilitate the process of realizing freedom to accept God's grace. In the end, Rahner's claim that God provides the condition that makes possible our freedom to love need not mean that God's grace ensures realization of this capacity in a way that is invulnerable to interpersonal harm.

Finally, it is important to revisit the relationship between grace, freedom, and salvation. In the end, does admitting the possibility that some may die before effecting a fundamental option undermine Rahner's central narrative that God creates us for the purpose of being able to freely choose communion with God by loving God and neighbor during this lifetime? This revised account of freedom and grace acknowledges the possibility that the efficacy of God's grace to enable a free human response to the divine self-offer may be compromised by human evil in the temporal sphere; it is indeed tragic and an ultimate affront to God's purposes for creation if interpersonal harm blocks effective mediation of grace and destroys a person's ability to effect a fundamental option before death. This does not mean, however, that God's grace is overcome by human evil in the ultimate sense of salvation. Our faith in God's goodness and justice grounds our belief that God will ultimately save persons in the event that they die before effecting a fundamental option. When reflecting on infants and others who lack reason and die before effecting a fundamental option, Rahner claims that God finds some way—perhaps after death—of making possible their free response to God's self-communication.

Conclusion

Having developed a revised Rahnerian theology of freedom and grace that more adequately attends to the realities of trauma survivors, it is now time to examine the ethical implications that result from embracing this revised theological anthropology. Such a revised account offers an empowering theological framework for trauma victims that fosters their recovery and ability to realize their freedom before God. It also has profound ethical implications for Christian communities, transforming Christian perceptions of what is at stake in how we are to love our neighbor and what form this love must take.

6

Ethical Directions

Implications of a Revised Theology of Freedom and Grace

Thus far, I have argued that an adequate account of God's grace and human freedom must be able to respond to the experiences of trauma victims and survivors. It must, therefore, acknowledge that interpersonal relations have the potential not only to damage (perhaps destroy) individuals' freedom for a fundamental option but also to mediate God's healing grace. The revised Rahnerian theology of freedom and grace articulated in chapter 5 has positive implications not only for faith and understanding but also for moral action. In this chapter, I turn specifically to the vast ethical implications that a revised Rahnerian theology has both for individuals and entire communities of faith. I will be particularly concerned with the following questions. How can this revised theology of grace and freedom actually help empower renewed agency for trauma survivors? How might it change the possible ethical and pastoral responses of faith communities (especially Christian communities) in relation to trauma victims and survivors? What new understandings (formative of and generated by the revised theology) need to be emphasized? What are the possibilities for transformation and how Christians perceive their obligation to love their neighbor?

Trauma Survivors: New Beliefs and New Possibilities

The revised understanding of the self, human freedom, and divine grace developed in chapter 5 has significant healing and liberating potential for trauma survivors. Attending to the seriousness of traumatization, it points to both resources and strategies that will aid survivors in a process of recovery. In order to appreciate this initially, imagine this revised understanding as part of the knowledge that informs an incest victim's faith community. Consider, for example, the acknowledgment that interpersonal harm can in fact severely damage the freedom of an individual to respond to God's grace. This acknowledgment alone can contribute to healing for incest victims because it begins to clarify for sexual abuse survivors the reasons they struggle with agency. Rather than blaming themselves for their abuse and resulting PTSD, incest victims can more easily understand that their behavioral reactions to the abuse are common and have even played a role in their survival. This perspective in itself might enable a victim to counter the overwhelming feelings of shame and self-hatred typically experienced by survivors. An individual could sense from interactions with others in the community that her struggle with a fractured self is intelligible in a communal context. She might thus feel understood, welcomed, and supported within the community rather than "different," abnormal, and isolated.

Moreover, we might hope that a community that addresses openly the potentially devastating effects of interpersonal harm on victims might attempt to prevent future abuse by empowering children and adolescents through knowledge of the causes, effects, and prevalence of abuse. Those currently being abused might, as a result, confide in religious leaders, allowing intervention and healing before further damage occurs.

One might object that a community's public acknowledgment of the radical vulnerability of individuals to interpersonal harm may actually work against prevention, healing, and recovery from sexual abuse: after all, it may be disempowering to consider openly the possibility that a person subject to overwhelming violence could die before effecting a fundamental option. Open attention to such possibilities could conceivably discourage victims and drive them to the despairing realization that they may already have been so harmed that they cannot actualize a "yes" to God's self-offer. In other words, could this revised understanding of God's grace and human freedom not exaggerate a sense of victimization and thereby disempower abuse survivors?

Such an objection seems implausible for two reasons. First, many incest victims already struggle with the fear that their perpetrators have destroyed their ability to love others and make healthy, constructive choices that will lead to recovery. What they need when experiencing such fear and despair is precisely the support from others who can offer understanding and consistent encouragement that healing and recovery from traumatization is possible. Thus, acknowledging the prospect of profound harm to one's freedom in a communal context does not introduce a new fear for traumatized persons; on the contrary, it demonstrates that a community takes seriously the extent to which persons can be debilitated by trauma and commits itself to help persons recover the essential abilities needed for agency and love.

Second, as Rahner acknowledges in "Christian Dying," the mystery of grace and freedom does not permit anyone to know whether such an abstract possibility of someone dying before effecting a fundamental option ever definitively occurs. It simply does not make sense to speculate whether such a possibility has occurred in concrete cases, or to despair about a living person's possible "inability" to effect a fundamental option. There is always hope for each and every living person to forge supportive relationships, actualize her freedom to accept God's grace, and continually deepen her "yes" to God's self-offer. This would be the message given in a faith community informed by understandings of freedom and grace such as I have proposed.

Let us now turn to explore how the insight that God mediates grace interpersonally can foster healing for incest survivors, particularly if they are working through feelings of betrayal and abandonment by God. The revised account of grace affirms that God, desiring to be intimately present to all persons, offers Godself from the very beginning of each person's existence; God's loving care never wavers. Unfortunately, however, abusive interpersonal relationships can obscure and actually damage incest victims' ability to perceive and trust in God's love—in two ways. If an incest victim has not experienced interpersonal love to a significant degree, a primary means by which God mediates grace has been blocked by others' sinful actions. In addition, the abuse and its posttraumatic effects can distort an incest victim's ability to perceive grace even when it is being offered by God. Since traumatization can thwart incest victims' ability to accept grace in a conscious sense, understanding that God's loving offer of self-communication is mediated historically and socially can help survivors better understand that God has never stopped bestowing grace on them. Rather, they may understand that experiences of chronic abuse have obscured God's love from being clearly manifested to them and have distorted their ability to perceive and trust in God's abiding love. Incest victims' profound suffering and alienation have been due to the effects of interpersonal harm rather than a lack of concern on God's behalf.

Furthermore, although God's grace obviously does not appear to work magically by shielding persons' freedom from interpersonal harm, this should not be taken to imply that God's self-offer does not positively alter each person's experience of who she is in conscious and unconscious ways. Without minimizing the fact that a significant percentage of incest victims do not survive, and the extent to which incest victims suffer, Rahner's theology of grace suggests the possibility that their existence could have been unimaginably worse were it not for their graced orientation toward God's self-offer. Although it remains a mystery how God's grace touches and transforms each person's existence, it is conceivable that the presence of grace has sustained incest victims in ways they are unaware of and has enabled them to survive the human cruelty and abuse to which they have been subjected. Within the context of pastoral counseling, abuse survivors can be encouraged to explore how God may have been present to them throughout the years in which they were abused. Some survivors believe that their very survival reflects God's loving care.[1]

Finally, understanding that one important way God mediates grace is through interpersonal relations empowers incest survivors to seek support from others and to be open to the mediation of God's love in interpersonal contexts. Incest survivors can recognize that the need to obtain social support is not a sign of personal weakness but a sign of responsibly pursuing the resources that foster one's healing and recovery. Recognizing that the development of capacities to act freely and constructively is a process dependent in part on supportive relationships with others, incest survivors may be motivated to seek out supportive persons in the community.

In summary, the revised theological anthropology outlined in chapter 5 may provide incest victims with hope that, given the experience of supportive relationships and the presence of God's mediating grace, they can experience healing from extreme interpersonal harm; they can regain (or in some cases develop for the first time) the ability to love and accept themselves, God, and their neighbor. Thus, far from undermining Rahner's emphasis on our freedom and responsibility before God, this revised account of God's grace and human freedom affirms that we are all responsible to seek help and be open to the presence of God's love in our interactions with others. Of course, everything I have suggested here regarding the possibilities for the prevention and healing of serious trauma remains contingent on whether or not communities do indeed respond wisely and with commitment to the problem of sexual abuse in their midst. What exactly are the particular possibilities and responsibilities of Christian communities?

Faith Communities: New Directions and Ethical Imperatives

Some important general ethical implications emerge from a revised theology of freedom and grace such as I have proposed. I limit my focus here to Christian communities, with particular reference to Roman Catholic communities, simply because the theology I have been working with—Karl Rahner's—is a Catholic Christian theology. This also allows me to employ some general assumptions about Christian (and Roman Catholic) meanings of church as community, and of the requirements for neighbor-love as well as love of God. Nonetheless, I trust that much of what I say here will provide analogies for the responses of other faith communities to the problems of traumatic sexual abuse.

First, it will come as no surprise if I identify new responsibilities for Christian neighbor-love that are grounded precisely in an obligation to foster one another's capacity for freedom before God. To explore these responsibilities, we need to appreciate the extent to which our self-descriptions shape and influence our behavior and moral aspirations. In the present case, of course, new self-descriptions are not arbitrary or whimsical but the result of insights into ourselves as we really function intersubjectively. As relationally constituted, embodied selves (rather than selves who simply possess an invulnerable core of freedom), we have the potential to foster or to debilitate one another's freedom to love.

In a very real sense, we can be collaborators with God in the affirmation and nurturance of one another's graced freedom. Insofar as this intersubjective nature of freedom characterizes our self-understanding, it can sharpen consciences, making it increasingly difficult to deny, minimize, or be apathetic about the prevalence of interpersonal harm among us and its devastating effects. This in turn can make us open to learning about the terrible destructiveness of prolonged sexual abuse and the consequent dynamics of PTSD. At the very least, our love for one another will lead us not to judge individuals who have suffered from severe interpersonal harm, blaming them for the ways they continue to reenact past trauma. More than this, persons who incorporate such understandings and attitudes into their commitments as Christians may experience an intensified moral imperative to intervene and aid individuals in realizing their freedom to love themselves, others, and God.

The implications of a revised theology of grace and freedom point in the same directions. The way we conceive of the relation between God's grace and human freedom also affects our perceptions of our responsibilities to one another. If we view God's grace as always directly enabling persons' freedom to love God and neighbor in a vertical fashion (i.e., without mediation by humans), we can, in the end, hold ourselves excused from any responsibility for others' plights. Insofar as we believe that whatever we do, our actions and their consequences have no *definitive* influence on others' freedom before God, we rest complacent in the assumption that God's grace will somehow ensure the possibility of every person's fundamental option to love God and neighbor. But if a primary way God mediates healing grace is through loving, interpersonal relationships, then Christ's call to love one's neighbor as oneself must be seen in a new light. It becomes increasingly clear that the command of neighbor-love is not only a command to demonstrate obedience and love for God. Neither are we called to love and risk ourselves for others solely or primarily for our own authentic self-realization. What is at stake in our daily decisions whether or not to love and how to love our neighbor is more far-reaching and profound: God calls us to love our neighbor because such love is needed to mediate divine grace. By loving others, we enable our neighbor's ability to accept freely God's offer of Christ, a choice that culminates in full communion with the divine. The process of effecting a fundamental option is ultimately more intersubjective and takes place communally in a deeper sense than the Christian tradition has frequently supposed.

Such emphasis on our responsibilities to foster each other's ability to effect a fundamental option for God accords deeply with Rahner's conception of the Church. As noted in the last chapter, Rahner conceives of the Church as making "the reality of salvation present" to each person, mediating God's transcendental self-offer in a "tangible and concrete way."[2] Underscoring that God mediates grace through supportive relationships, however, offers greater specificity about exactly how grace is communicated, broadening the notion of sacramentality within the life of the Church. Consequently, greater attention is placed on how each member of the Church plays a vital role in making present the reality of salvation effected by Christ.

Identifying the deep intersubjectivity of freedom also has implications for our understanding of sin and guilt, and this in turn suggests further responsibilities for Christian communities. Studies on trauma consistently find that the duration of a trauma and the communal response once it is exposed and stopped are two central factors affecting the degree to which one's sense of self and agency becomes debilitated. The presence or absence of supportive relationships, in other words, is a crucial variable for recovery. Such studies have shown that children who report incestuous abuse before it becomes chronic and who receive support from their nonoffending parents and others do not experience nearly the same degree of traumatization as those who are chronically abused.[3] In fact, many of the children who receive immediate validation and therapy do not suffer from posttraumatic stress symptoms at all.[4] Such research has important implications for Christian communities, indicating that they have real influence over the extent of harm resulting from sexual abuse, particularly for children who are members of their congregations. While Christian communities may not be able to eradicate child sexual abuse, they do have the power and hence the responsibility to take important steps to prevent it. By the same token, they have a responsibility to increase abused children's prospects of recovery and to mitigate the harm they suffer. Thus, a community that embraces the revised theology of freedom and grace articulated in chapter 5 may be expected to emphasize that sins of omission threaten our positive response to God as much as actively sinning against others.

This last insight underscores the importance of traditional connections between actively harming someone and passively allowing harm to occur. We might even say that onlookers, doing nothing to intervene or prevent recognized abuse, find themselves in a blurry continuum of evil at a point that begins to approach (although obviously not equal) the evil of the abuser. Recognizing the ways that we actually participate in the ongoing abuse and traumatization of children due to our inactions resulting from ignorance, indifference, or complacency resonates with Rahner's emphasis on the social nature of sin and guilt. Rahner would argue that each person's failure to take proactive steps in preventing sexual abuse is codetermined by the guilt of others in history and in the present. Appreciating how "our own freedom bears the stamp of the guilt of others in a way which cannot be eradicated" equips us to understand better why it is so difficult to overcome indifference and motivates us to consider thoroughly the constructive steps we may take to prevent abuse.[5]

Finally, this revised understanding has implications for how we interpret the relation between a Christian commitment to liberation (seeking to free persons from oppression and other forms of suffering) and the Christian meaning of salvation. There is, of course, a diversity of views about the relationship between worldly liberation and salvation. Although it is beyond the scope of this book to treat the many theological disputes about worldly liberation, eschatology, the Kingdom of God, and salvation, I simply wish to point out the relevance of a revised Rahnerian theological anthropology to this set of issues. Within the framework of this revised account, striving for social justice would attempt to ensure as far as is possible that salvation for every person occurs the way God most desires—through an interplay of divine and human freedom. As noted in chapter 2, Rahner goes so far as to assert:

> This salvation takes place as the salvation of a free person, as the fulfillment of a free person as such, and hence it takes place precisely when this person, in fact, actualizes himself in freedom, that is, towards his salvation. It never takes place without the involvement of the person and his freedom. A salvation not achieved in freedom cannot be salvation.[6]

From this point of view, one among many reasons Christian communities should strive for greater social justice is that liberation from oppression provides conditions—minimal well-being and an environment that fosters supportive relations rather than dehumanizing ones—that may in fact be needed to realize one's freedom to effect a fundamental option. The tentative nature of the phrase "may be needed" communicates, of course, that we have no way of knowing with certainty whether such conditions are strictly necessary. We do know with certainty, however, that healing made possible through supportive interpersonal relationships frees persons to love in ways that are not possible when they are imprisoned within the dynamics of traumatization.

Specific Forms of Neighbor-Love: Mediating the Graces of Survival

Thus far, I have argued that, according to the Christian tradition, God's grace frees us to love God and neighbor, and recognizing the socially mediated dimensions of God's grace heightens our sense of obligation toward our neighbor. Furthermore, reaching out in love to those suffering in our midst (such as sexual abuse victims) may be moments whereby God communicates grace, freeing persons from the paralyzing grip of traumatization, and making possible their freedom to love themselves, God, and others. The general contours of Rahner's theological ethics are clear, but what specific forms of neighbor-love can best respond to the needs of sexual abuse survivors? An obvious way to begin this discernment process is to consider how Christian communities can accompany and support survivors as they negotiate their way through the three general stages that are often associated with recovery from sexual violence: reestablishing a sense of bodily and environmental safety within their own bodies and their surrounding environment, naming and "confronting" the past abuse, and reconnecting with ordinary life.[7]

Welcoming to a Safe Space

Christian communities must be committed to several important steps if they are effectively to provide a safe and welcoming environment for sexual abuse survivors. An initial step is to acknowledge, apologize, and repent for past failures to provide a safe haven for violated children and women, a sanctuary in which justice and healing could have been sought. Although many Christian denominations have condemned sexual violence in formal church documents,[8] they have barely begun pastorally to acknowledge the prevalence of sexual violence and its devastating effects and to take proactive steps to address it. As the recent child sexual abuse crisis in the Catholic Church unfortunately demonstrates, silence, secrecy, and coverups have rendered Christian communities complicit in the denial and minimization of sexual violence and its consequences.[9] Failing to raise consciousness about debilitating effects of sexual and domestic abuse has made it easier for perpetrators to continue their crimes against those most vulnerable, in many cases maintaining their Christian identity as they do so.

Historically, remaining silent and ignoring the ongoing violence against women and children has not been the only failure on the part of Christian churches to pursue justice and healing. Sexually violated women and children have frequently reported that clergy have turned a deaf ear to their cries for help and intervention. Some of the most typical responses to sexual abuse victims include refusing to believe the abuse, minimizing its harmfulness, blaming victims and telling them to confess their sins, sympathizing with the abuser, and/or sexually abusing the victims themselves.[10] Consider, for example, one priest's immediate response to an instance of a reported sexual abuse: "I feel so sorry for your father; think what all of this must be doing to him."[11] Such responses retraumatize the sexual abuse victims in varying degrees while reinforcing their self-hatred, shame, and alienation.

Christian clergy have also failed to help perpetrators confront their violence and change their behavior. In the rare instances in which perpetrators have come forward and confessed sexual/physical violence, clergy frequently have not (for the supposed reason of maintaining confidentiality) reported the violence to public authorities.[12] Instead, church leaders have tended to view such violence as a private sin, and they have focused on forgiving the perpetrators and sending them home—actions that did not fundamentally challenge or alter the abusive behavior.[13] In fact, a study involving twenty-five incest offenders reported that the least helpful clergy response to sexual abuse is immediate forgiveness; praying over the offender and forgiving him prior to expressions of repentance minimize the violence and fail to hold the perpetrator publicly accountable for his abuse.[14]

Why have Christian communities so often failed to offer a safe, supportive environment for sexual abuse survivors, stopping short of providing consolation, pastoral assistance, and shared efforts for justice? It is beyond the scope of this chapter to provide a thorough response to this question. Yet there are at least two general problems that go a long way toward explaining these failures: problems of faith (or more properly, of understandings of faith) and problems of justice in practice. I will address these briefly, attempting to show the need for transformation within community.

TRANSFORMING BELIEFS. The Christian tradition has been marked by ambivalence regarding issues of violence against children and women, and this ambivalence has been rooted in biblical and theological texts. Feminist critiques of these interpretations are widespread,[15] so a few brief examples will be sufficient. Although there are biblical passages that condemn rape, incest, and violence, and that affirm an obligation to protect and provide for the most vulnerable, the Bible also contains many passages that justify and legitimate patriarchal beliefs and practices that implicitly or even explicitly sanction violence against women and children. For instance, Ezekiel, Hosea, and Jeremiah depict God as a jealous husband who justifiably acts violently toward his wife Israel.[16] In her analysis of the texts with this imagery, Renita Weems elaborates:

> Like a jealous husband who has been humiliated by his wife's affairs, God was capable of taking some unimaginably harsh measures against Israel his wife. God is described as an abusive husband who batters his wife, strips her naked, and leaves her to be raped by her lovers, only to take her back in the end, insisting that when all is said and done Israel the wife shall remain interminably the wife of an abusing husband.... Here the prophets admitted that Israel's history had shown repeatedly that God was as capable of being abusive as God was of being compassionate.[17]

The Hebrew scriptures also contain terrifying narratives of fathers committing violence against their daughters. In two separate instances, a father offers his daughter to be raped by a mob of men to protect the safety of a male guest.[18] In another story, Jephthah kills his daughter to fulfill a vow to God. Remarkably, neither of these men is condemned by God for such acts. Stories like this have undoubtedly legitimized (or at least failed to challenge) violence against women.

Likewise, many well-known passages in the New Testament validate patriarchal authoritarianism and exhort women to submit to and obey their husbands.[19] Historically, many theologians (as well as abusive husbands)[20] have appealed to such passages either to justify physical and sexual violence or to argue that women must acquiesce and endure the abuse.[21]

Furthermore, theologians and ministers have interpreted core theological doctrines in ways that have functioned if not to legitimize abuse, then at least to maintain it in practice. Consider dominant interpretations of the suffering and death of Jesus that emphasize his selfless death for the sins of others in obedience to God's will. Numerous theologians have expressed concern that atonement imagery has (unwittingly or not) sanctioned divine child abuse—the Father sacrificing the Son for the redemption of all.[22] Moreover, the belief that Christians are called to imitate Christ's willingness to sacrifice out of love for others, and in obedience to God, has sometimes exacerbated the dynamics of victimization. Certain theologians and therapists argue that women and children, applying these theological beliefs to their abusive situations, often become convinced that God's will is realized by "bearing their cross" and selflessly putting the needs of the family (needs defined by the abuser) before their own. Since Christ's suffering was redemptive, and one ought to imitate Christ's example of selflessness, meekness, and humility, there appears no legitimate path to redemption in their context that does not include simply suffering as a result of ongoing violence.[23]

Christian views about forgiveness within the sacred bond of marriage and the family constitute another traditional theological tenet that has disempowered many abused women and children. Exhorting sexual abuse victims to forgive and forget the actions of their perpetrators has been a common refrain. Violated women have been exhorted to imitate Jesus' acceptance of suffering and forgive "seventy times seven."[24] Unfortunately, certain clergypersons still promulgate this thinking. The evangelist Bill Gothard's counsel to battered women is typical of this mindset. When asked how he responds to women who are victims of their husbands' battering, he says,

> There is no victim if we understand that we are called to suffer for righteousness. For even hereunto were ye called because Christ also suffered for us, leaving us an example that ye should follow in his steps (1 Peter 3:4).... Christ was not a victim, he willingly gave his life for us.... By his stripes ye were healed (1 Peter 2:24).... Likewise ye wives (1 Peter 3:1).[25]

The imperative to forgive unconditionally and to keep one's family intact at all costs has functioned to keep many women and children imprisoned within the abusive dynamics of their homes, often leaving their very lives in peril.[26] In the end, interpretations of central Christian convictions and doctrines have all too often failed to equip women and children with the resources to resist violence effectively; at their worst, many common interpretations have legitimized the violence itself.

Fortunately, many theologians have criticized these biblical passages and interpretations of theological doctrines during the last half of the twentieth century.[27] Alternative interpretations of biblical passages and doctrines have been proposed that empower marginalized persons to resist violence and oppression and experience healing. It is difficult, of course, to know how influential these constructive theological texts have been in transforming beliefs of local Christian communities. The fact that many Christian incest survivors continue to hold problematic interpretations of theological beliefs that thwart their healing demonstrates that full-scale transformation of beliefs in Christian communities remains incomplete.[28]

TRANSFORMING PRACTICES. Along with problematic understandings of biblical texts and theological traditions, the practices of church members—including ministers, counselors, clergy, and laypersons—have forestalled aggressive action to prevent and heal sexual abuse. Far from preventing abuse and fostering healing, a significant percentage of Christian ministers and clergy have themselves sexually violated women and children in their own congregations.[29] As of December 2003, 4 percent of Catholic priests from 1950 to 2002 were accused of sexually abusing a minor.[30] This covert practice of sexual violation has undoubtedly contributed (and for many Christian communities continues to contribute) to the tendency to avoid the issue of sexual violence, fail to condemn it, and prophetically seek its eradication throughout society. Although it is unclear historically how pervasive this abuse has been, numerous reported cases of clergy sexual misconduct in the last forty years make it painfully clear that such abuse is no stranger to any of the Christian denominations or other religious communities.[31] Failing to prevent the violation of women and children (both boys and girls) in their midst, many Christian communities have even tended to protect perpetrators. Just as an incestuous father typically continues to commit sexual violence through secrecy, denial, and threats, an alarming number of Christian authorities across denominational boundaries have sought to conceal incidents of sexual abuse, and have silenced its victims through various means.[32] The recent explosion of clergy sexual abuse cases in the Roman Catholic Church is a dramatic example of these deeply ingrained, tragic dynamics.

Christian communities, in light of the obstacles that have kept them from effectively addressing the problem of sexual violence, now have several courses of action before them if they are to fashion safe and welcoming places for abuse survivors. First among these is profound repentance for all the ways that faith communities (including their own) have failed sexually abused members. In particular, careful attention must be given to the needs of survivors abused by their own clergy. This must be followed by compassion; just restitution to victims, which includes communal acknowledgment of the abuse, financial compensation for costs related to recovery, and so on; and holding perpetrators accountable for their actions.

In addition to reporting clergy sexual abuse to public authorities, Christian churches must take appropriate measures to ensure as far as humanly possible the prevention of further sexual abuse and misconduct by clergy and other adults. Moving in this direction, the Catholic Church in the United States has begun implementing, in all of their dioceses, *Protecting God's Children*—a program that trains children, adolescents, parents, ministers, church employees, and volunteers to ensure a child-safe environment, detect warning signs of child abuse, and prevent further abuse. As of December 31, 2004, 94 percent of Catholic dioceses were compliant with all of the provisions of the Catholic Church's *Charter for the Protection of Children and Young People.*[33]

Besides these concrete steps to make the Church a safe space, communities need to question which of their current beliefs, attitudes, and practices undermine their resolve to offer an environment where justice and healing can occur. This returns us to considerations noted in the previous section. It is, after all, impossible to separate belief from practice. Self-critical inquiry must take place at various levels. For instance, besides reexamining structural sexist practices that contribute to the formation of perpetrators, Christian churches need to become more sensitive to the potential for certain scriptural passages, theological doctrines, and liturgical practices to retraumatize sexual abuse survivors. The following questions are just a sampling of the theological issues that communities must resolve: Which divine images and names help foster trust in God and healing? Which, by contrast, result in fear and emotional numbing? How can the celebration of the Eucharist avoid being interpreted as a traumatic reenactment of violence? Which liturgical practices and healing services are empowering, not threatening, to sexual abuse survivors?

Christian communities also need to profess in a multitude of ways that they acknowledge and condemn the pervasive reality of sexual violence within their communities and throughout society. They must give priority to the education of their leaders and communities about the prevalence of child sexual abuse in our society and its devastating effects on victims. Positive practical strategies abound: pamphlets about sexual violence, for example, and information about sources of support can be posted in visible areas in churches; resources can be obtained from such organizations as the Faith Trust Institute and the Interfaith Sexual Trauma Institute;[34] and books and videotapes can be placed in church libraries. If they do not sponsor their own educational forums on abuse, denominations can send their clergy and interested church members to conferences and workshops. Since insufficient research exists on the complex issues related to religion and sexual violence, Christian denominations might also collaborate with one another and with other religious traditions to establish additional centers (like the two mentioned) dedicated to research and education regarding these issues.

Finally, cultivating a safe environment involves striving for justice with and for sexual abuse survivors. According to Marie Fortune, founder of the Faith Trust Institute, actualizing justice for abuse survivors begins by acknowledging to the abuse victim and her community that he or she has been unjustly harmed.[35] The prior steps of condemning the prevalence of sexual abuse and listening to and supporting the survivor are effective ways to communicate that unjust violations have occurred and that survivors are not to blame. In a situation where sexual abuse is currently occurring, clergy obviously need to report the sexual violence to public authorities, offer adequate pastoral support to the victim's family, and refer victims to religious and secular social services to ensure their safety. When possible, the community should confront the perpetrator and seek to hold him or her accountable for the abuse. When considering adult sexual abuse survivors dealing with past memories of abuse, communities can help them secure resources needed for healing, especially when perpetrators fail to provide restitution to facilitate a survivor's recovery.[36]

Inevitably, raising consciousness about justice for sexual abuse survivors will motivate many church members to use their own particular gifts to prevent and eradicate sexual violence: they will want, among other things, to provide a supportive presence for survivors who are pursuing justice through the court system, volunteer at local crisis centers and shelters, educate adults and children about sexual abuse, and seek to change laws and social practices that protect perpetrators and retraumatize victims. Thus, seeking to help victims meet their needs, demanding accountability from abusers, preventing abusers from harming others, and creating right relationships with survivors and perpetrators paves a road for justice and authentic healing.[37]

Addressing the Past

By offering a safe and supportive environment for sexual abuse survivors, churches will have laid the necessary groundwork for further forms of support, as survivors seek to remember and piece together their (often fragmented) memories of trauma and mourn the abuse and its lasting effects. This is the second stage of recovery. In her work *Redeeming Memories*, Flora Keshgegian points out that the very process of remembering can only occur within a supportive, interpersonal context.[38] She envisions Christian communities drawing on their rich liturgical and theological resources as they offer a sacred space in which the Church listens openly and affirms the process of remembering trauma: "The church's witness . . . is one of listening—listening to the sometimes barely audible and emerging voices of those who have been victimized."[39]

Strong support at this stage of recovery is crucial. Since remembering is accompanied by all of the unbearably negative emotions that have been repressed for years, this period of articulating one's fragmented memories and telling others about one's abusive past is usually the most painful stage of recovery. Many survivors feel intense depression and despair; many even become suicidal. As they struggle conceptually to piece together their abusive past, survivors usually need to tell their story repeatedly to persons who are willing to listen, who will believe their excruciatingly painful memories, and who are willing to grieve with them. As the therapist Midge Finley, director of the incest support group Victims of Incest Recovering through Understanding, Education, and Support (VIRTUES) observes: "We human beings are all too fragile to bear grief alone, which is why grieving as a community is so important."[40]

While support groups and relationships with a therapist, family, and friends are invaluable for survivors' recovery process, a Christian community offers a unique source of support that especially aids survivors as they confront spiritual losses and seek to reconstruct their faith and relation to God. By sharing their stories with the community and laying their abusive memories in the hands of God, there is hope that abuse survivors' stories of violence and affliction will be transformed within the context of Jesus' own experiences of crucifixion and resurrection.[41] Just as Christian churches preserve and uphold the memories of Jesus' experiences of betrayal and abandonment, his crucifixion, and his resurrection, so, too, can they validate survivors' memories of violation and traumatization. As Rahner argues, belief in Christ's resurrection can enable Christians to confront with courage the bitterest aspects of human reality—by listening to stories of severe human cruelty and vulnerability, for example—and to repeatedly express hope that greater healing and redemption will also occur for the survivor.

In order to bear witness to survivors during this period of remembering and mourning, Christian communities can express their solidarity for survivors in communal ways. Through liturgical rituals, communal prayer, and singing, small groups or perhaps the entire community can publicly mourn the losses and suffering resulting from sexual violence. Communities might also honor the forms of resistance and resilience that have enabled traumatized persons' survival. Victims who have not survived sexual abuse should also be lifted up and remembered during these times, particularly in communal prayers. Overall, many sexual abuse survivors in this stage of recovery experience liturgical rituals such as the laying on of hands as powerful moments to experience healing.[42] Such rituals, rich in symbolism and creativity, can help to heal one's body and spirit in ways that are often more effective than the direct forms of communication that occur in counseling and daily conversations. In her book *Take and Make Holy*, sexual abuse survivor Mari Zimmerman offers descriptions of healing services that include themes such as validating one's commitment to the healing process, cleansing one's self from feelings of shame, mourning one's lost childhood, reconciling oneself with God, and celebrating new images of God.[43]

Of course, communities must be wary of the prospect of retraumatizing sexual abuse survivors during healing rituals. There always exists the danger that such rituals can trigger flashbacks of the abuse, hyperarousal, and emotional numbing. Perhaps participants in these healing services should be limited to sexual abuse survivors and those who support them. When more inclusive healing services are offered to the entire community, it is crucial for sexual abuse (and other trauma) survivors to participate in planning the healing liturgy and to have the opportunity to review its contents before attending the service.

Christian communities can mediate God's love and acceptance of the abuse survivor by asking him or her to participate in liturgical rituals during church services. This simple act communicates to the survivor that she is capable and worthy of manifesting God's presence and grace to the congregation. For instance, an incest survivor named "Lauren" emphasized how stunned she felt when she was asked to be a regular reader during the liturgy.[44] Feeling completely "dirty," worthless, and ashamed, she had not thought that she was worthy of communicating the Word of God to others. Yet such a simple request on the part of the Christian community conveyed to Lauren that God viewed her as good and holy. This experience of being "sanctified"[45] within a religious community directly opposed the experiences of sexual abuse, particularly the inherent powerlessness and debasement of being treated as the object of another's gratification.

In addition to communal forms of worship and prayer, Christian communities must offer adequate pastoral support. While religious leaders should acknowledge the limitations of their pastoral training and refer incest survivors to pastoral counselors who specialize in recovery from trauma, they must also recognize the invaluable source of support they can provide in the healing process. Pastoral counselor Molly Brown recommends that clergy, teachers, and other religious leaders (parish administrators or associates, retreat leaders, religious education teachers, prayer-group facilitators, etc.) receive training on how to listen to the pain of sexual abuse victims, support them in their daily lives, and help them obtain the counseling they may need.[46] In times of severe despair, such advocates can offer hope that survivors will at some point be freed of gripping anxiety and depression, and instead experience love and joy. With these advocates, survivors can perhaps for the first time shed their "false selves" and begin to share how they really view themselves. Victim advocates can mirror all the good attributes they witness in survivors, supporting their emerging "authentic" selves and growing capacity for effective agency.

Survivors also need advocates, ministers, and pastoral counselors who are willing to accompany them as they confront their spiritual losses resulting from sexual abuse. They need to begin to reconstruct their religious faith. Being present to survivors as they express the rage, betrayal, and grief they feel toward God can therefore be another way of mediating God's steadfast love and acceptance. While being wise enough not to offer insensitive solutions or simplified theological answers, such advocates can share appropriate personal insights and theological resources as they discern together with survivors the presence of God in their lives. Mari Zimmerman expresses the invaluable impact such support has on survivors during their process of remembering and grieving:

> We feel the warmth of God's love radiating from those who love us even when we cannot love ourselves. They show us the faithfulness of God when we pray. We are given hope by those who refuse to let us go even when we slide into the depths of despair. Places of safety become the holy places where we experience God in our lives.[47]

Ultimately, the hope is that pastoral support can, as Brown argues, "aid [survivors] in finding their way back from soul murder to a compassionate church."[48]

Christian communities, of course, should by no means think they have a monopoly on insights for recovery. On the contrary, the discussion and work necessary for a climate of recovery likely improves in proportion to a church's openness to, and collaboration with, a wealth of conversation partners. Collaborating with other religious and secular groups, churches can, for example, pool resources to provide support groups for the benefit of all who are in the midst of remembering and mourning their abuse. Such groups offer a unique way for survivors to forge trusting and empathetic relationships, finding within themselves additional strengths to aid them in healing. Churches that have sponsored religious retreats and conferences focused on healing from sexual abuse have also offered survivors unique opportunities for greater spiritual and psychological healing.[49]

Through various processes of integrating the trauma narrative into their overall life histories and grieving losses within the context of supportive relationships, survivors gradually experience a lessening of the intensity of traumatic memories. They begin to feel freed from the hold that the traumatic injuries have had on them. At this point in their journey, some survivors feel able to forgive their perpetrator.[50] Many therapists and survivors describe forgiveness as a last step in the process of letting go, as no longer being bound by the trauma.[51] Reconciliation in this life, however, may not be possible, especially since the vast majority of incest perpetrators are unwilling to admit their abuse and express repentance. Whether or not a survivor identifies this process of "letting go" as forgiveness, the theological significance of this moment cannot be exaggerated. Since the task of surviving the effects of traumatic memories and posttraumatic symptoms no longer saps all of the survivor's energy on a daily basis, she now is able to direct much of her attention to "ordinary life" concerns. These include a myriad of concrete ways of relating with love to herself, others, and God. We now turn to the role that the Christian community can play in this last stage of recovery.

Companioning Forward to Ordinary Life

Christian communities can also be an invaluable resource for survivors in their last stage of recovery—reconnecting with ordinary life. During this time, survivors' tasks are to develop a healthy sense of self, forge new relationships, and achieve an effective sense of agency within their lives. There exists in the Church a wealth of opportunities for fellowship and growth in relationships with other persons and God. For example, survivors can become involved in social justice projects, teach religious education, plan and participate in the liturgy, or join a choir, small church community, or Bible study group. Such activities open survivors' horizons and help free them further from preoccupation with past trauma; consequently, they can begin to appreciate and take joy in the ordinary details of life. As they develop healthy friendships within the community, survivors can practice setting boundaries, sharing ideas and aspirations, and fashioning new identities. One sexual abuse survivor, Susan, became involved in children's liturgy classes at her church.[52] Besides receiving positive feedback from the children and their parents and feeling a sense of pride in her accomplishments, Susan forged friendships with several of the parents and was able to develop her social skills in different contexts. Her own reflections with the children about God prompted her to find a spiritual director to explore further how to heal her relationship with God. In ways such as these, survivors with the support of a spiritual community are given the resources to discern how they have responded to God's self-communication in the past; this in turn prepares them to actualize more fully their "yes" to God's self-offer in the present and future.

Of course, many more practical examples for shepherding survivors once again into "ordinary life" can be identified. It suffices for the purposes of this book simply to point to these few examples. The possibilities thus identified should lead to clarity regarding ethical imperatives. These in turn can lead to creative work that goes beyond the scope of this project.

The Need for Caution

As I attempt to elucidate the aforementioned forms of neighbor-love, I do so with some concern. That is, espousing such pastoral suggestions may imply that a communal response to trauma is straightforward and easy. After all, how difficult can it possibly be to educate communities about sexual violence, listen to and offer support to survivors, and witness their process of recovery and healing? My own interactions with an incest survivor named "Lauren," which involved listening to her painful recollections and seeing how the incestuous abuse has reverberated throughout her life, compels me to add that the simple choice to accompany survivors, communally or individually, requires wisdom, patience, courage, and faith.

During the hours I sat listening to Lauren, there were moments when I had to fight the urge literally to flee. To my surprise, I experienced my teeth chattering at the end of certain interviews even when we sat outside on warm, sunny days. I also experienced extreme anger and grief on the days and even weeks after my interviews took place. To listen to and believe survivors' accounts of subjection to such severe interpersonal harm and its devastating effects can be excruciating, for it conflicts with our most comforting assumptions about the world and God. To embark on this journey with survivors involves a willingness to disrupt our sense of well-being, comfort, and security, and to be challenged in our view of ourselves, our world, and God.

Furthermore, it is necessary to let go of our own desires for survivors to resolve their trauma within our imposed time frame. Trauma survivors experience counterproductive frustration at the pressure placed on them by well-meaning loved ones and friends to "recover" from their trauma quickly.[53] Pressure like this minimizes the extent of damage undergone, and it can actually create an increased sense of alienation and shame. Due to such pressure, some incest survivors reject altogether the terms "healing" and "recovery." There is seldom any recovery that takes place in a linear sequence with a clear, final endpoint. While therapists and survivors have identified stages in the process of healing, resolution of the trauma is hardly ever final. Many survivors revisit their struggles with posttraumatic stress symptoms during different stages of their lives, especially during moments of increased stress. It is a chilling but true fact that a significant percentage of trauma survivors commit suicide even after many years of persistent effort. According to Lauren, many incest survivors (including herself) continually reassure themselves that suicide is a viable option if circumstances become finally unbearable.

In our decision to reach out in love to trauma victims, we must be aware that there are no assurances of triumphant "happy endings." Despite communities' or individuals' most sincere attempts to love and to facilitate a healing process, we still simply do not know the extent to which the wounds and scars of unspeakable human cruelty can in any given case be healed. Given the revised Rahnerian theology of freedom and grace that I have articulated in chapter 5, however, there remains the imperative for Christian communities to try to respond to the injuries in their midst. And it is surely true that many communities have not yet begun to realize their potential to mediate divine grace for prevention, survival, and recovery. With a revised understanding of freedom that adequately attends to trauma survivors' experiences, communities can hope that their acts of love and justice have the potential to mediate divine grace, fostering survivors' freedom to love themselves, others, and God.

Conclusion

As we have seen, the compulsion of severely traumatized persons to reenact past trauma, as well as their struggle to love themselves, others, and God, calls into question the credibility of Christian theologies that posit persons' invulnerable freedom for ultimate self-disposal. In this book, I have critically examined whether a theological anthropology like Karl Rahner's has adequate resources to recognize and address the dynamics of traumatization. Drawing on insights from trauma and feminist theory concerning human vulnerability, the social construction of the self, and conditions necessary for effective agency, I have argued that Rahner's construal of the self, freedom, and divine grace found in his most well-known writings fails to acknowledge sufficiently the extent to which interpersonal harm can threaten one's freedom to effect a fundamental option. The degree of utter brokenness and fragmentation manifested in the lives of traumatized victims shatters the ease with which any theology can sustain the assumption that persons inevitably have freedom to respond to God's grace, no matter how severe their experience of interpersonal harm.

Synthesizing insights from trauma survivors' experiences, feminist theory, and Rahner's lesser known and more pastoral writings, however, I have proposed that a revised Rahnerian theology of freedom can adequately respond to these contemporary challenges as long as it embraces two key insights. First, it must acknowledge the possibility that interpersonal harm can destroy a person's ability to respond freely to God's grace. Second, it must highlight the idea that a primary way God mediates grace is through loving, interpersonal relations.

Throughout this book, I suggested that there is much at stake ethically in the particular beliefs that Christian communities hold about freedom and grace. For this reason, articulating an adequate theology of freedom that remains true to a variety of human experiences is essential. A Christian theology of freedom that ignores or underemphasizes the effects of experiences such as severe traumatization not only fails to foster recovery from trauma; it may even reinforce societal tendencies of denial in the face of these experiences. Furthermore, insofar as a theology of freedom is insensitive to evidence from trauma studies and unwilling to consider insights from feminist theories, it may allow us to oversimplify the dynamics of trauma, and to blame victims for their compulsive, traumatic reenactments. We thereby stigmatize victims further, increasing their deeply entrenched shame and self-hatred and isolating them from communal support. Failing to articulate an adequate theology of freedom exacerbates the vicious cycle of traumatization and thwarts the potential of Christian communities to fulfill their purpose of mediating God's love to each person, ultimately sharing in God's plan of salvation.

By contrast, a theology of freedom that recognizes the power of interpersonal relations both to damage a person's capacity to respond to grace and to mediate God's grace heightens our sense of interpersonal responsibility for our neighbor. It helps us discern how to love in ways that foster one another's freedom to love. Although we cannot be assured of "happy endings" as we behold survivors' processes of healing and recovery, we can trust in the reports of many trauma survivors who testify to the healing power that loving relations offer. Given a revised Rahnerian theology of freedom, communities and individuals can coherently interpret the requirements of neighbor-love as I have tried to articulate them both generally and concretely here. With a theology that is adequate both to revelation and to experience, they can persist in the Christian hope that acts of love and justice have the potential to mediate divine grace, fostering trauma survivors' freedom to love themselves, others, and God.

Notes

CHAPTER I

1. At the center of Rahner's theology of freedom lies his formulation of the fundamental option: each person, with the aid of divine grace, has the freedom to realize a "yes" to God's self-offer by loving God and one's neighbor throughout one's lifetime or a "no" to God by choosing a life marked by egoism and selfishness.

2. Bessel van der Kolk and Alexander McFarlane, "The Black Hole of Trauma," in *Traumatic Stress*, ed. Bessel van der Kolk, Alexander McFarlane, and Lars Weisaeth (New York: Guilford Press, 1996), 5.

3. Intrusive memories can be experienced cognitively, affectively, and/or physiologically.

4. Van der Kolk and McFarlane, "Black Hole of Trauma," 6–7.

5. Alexander McFarlane and Bessel van der Kolk, "Trauma and Its Challenge to Society," in van der Kolk et al., *Traumatic Stress*, 43.

6. Ibid., 27–35. For more discussion about how American society continues to blame trauma victims in various ways, see Rebecca Coffey, *Unspeakable Truths and Happy Endings: Human Cruelty and the New Trauma Therapy* (Lutherville, Md.: Sidran Press, 1998); Jennifer Manlowe, *Faith Born of Seduction: Sexual Trauma, Body Image and Religion* (New York: New York University Press, 1995); M. J. Lerner, *The Belief in a Just World* (New York: Plenum Press, 1989); Christine Gudorf, *Victimization: Examining Christian Complacency* (Philadelphia: Trinity Press International, 1992).

7. See Alexander C. McFarlane, "The Severity of Trauma," in *Beyond Trauma*, ed. Rolf J. Kleber, Charles R. Figley, and Berthold P. R. Gersons (New York: Plenum Press, 1995), 48; George Everly, "Psychotraumatology," in *Psychotraumatology*, ed. George Everly and Jeffrey Lating (New York:

Plenum Press, 1995), 5; Jeffrey Means, *Trauma and Evil* (Minneapolis: Augsburg Fortress Press, 2000), 67–68.

8. Van der Kolk and McFarlane, "Black Hole of Trauma," 25.

9. Derek Summerfield, "Addressing Human Response to War and Atrocity," in Kleber et al., *Beyond Trauma,* 17–30. See also Mary Gilfus, "The Price of the Ticket: A Survivor-Centered Appraisal of Trauma Theory," *Violence Against Women* 5, 11 (1999): 1238–1258.

10. Certain authors suggest that racism, classism, and heterosexism constitute another form of trauma that needs to be addressed just as much as "circumscribed" traumas. See Maria Root, "Reconstructing the Impact of Trauma on Personality," in *Personality and Psychopathology: Feminist Reappraisals,* ed. Laura Brown and Mary Ballou (New York: Guilford Press, 1992), 229–266.

11. Thomas Aquinas, *Summa Theologiae* (New York: Benziger, 1948), I–II q.114 a.10. For further discussion, see John Bowlin, *Contingency and Fortune in Aquinas's Ethics* (New York: Cambridge University Press, 1999).

12. Aquinas, *Summa Theologiae,* I–II q.73 a.8.

13. Søren Kierkegaard, *The Journals of Søren Kierkegaard,* ed. and trans. Alexander Dru (London: Oxford University Press, 1959), 361–362. For further discussion, see Gene Outka, "On Harming Others," *Interpretation* 34, 4 (October 1980): 381–393, "Equality and the Fate of Theism in Modern Culture," *Journal of Religion* (July 1987): 275–288, and "Equality and Individuality: Thoughts on Two Themes in Kierkegaard," *Journal of Religious Ethics* (fall 1982): 171–203.

14. For theologians who believe that God's grace alone ensures a person's faith in Christ and, ultimately, their salvation, the experiences of traumatized persons may raise questions about the efficacy of God's grace and issues of predestination. As we will see in later chapters, many incest survivors, for instance, experience difficulty having faith in and trusting God. How would such theologians interpret these experiences? Does lack of faith demonstrate that God does not offer the grace of faith in Christ, or does it signal a failure of God's grace to overcome the debilitating effects of trauma?

15. These responses may not necessarily be directly occasioned by interpretations of trauma. Although thinkers may not specifically refer to trauma, it seems apparent that traumatic events are included within their definitions of interpersonal harm as well as the events that precipitate radical suffering.

16. Outka, "On Harming Others," 383.

17. Ibid.

18. Timothy Jackson, "Arminian Edification: Kierkegaard on Grace and Free Will," in *The Cambridge Companion to Kierkegaard,* ed. Alastair Hannay and Gordon D. Marino (Cambridge: Cambridge University Press, 1998), 243.

19. Ibid., 245.

20. Weil prefers the term "affliction" to denote radical suffering.

21. Simone Weil, *Waiting for God* (New York: Putnam, 1951), 119.

22. Ibid., 120.

23. Dorothee Soelle, *Suffering* (Philadelphia: Fortress Press, 1975), 2.

24. Ibid., 68–69.

25. Wendy Farley, *Tragic Vision and Divine Compassion* (Louisville, Ky.: Westminster, 1990), 2.

26. Ibid., 153–154.

27. Ibid., 59.

28. Weil, *Waiting for God*, 122–123.

29. Farley, *Tragic Vision and Divine Compassion*, 58.

30. Marjorie Suchocki, *The Fall to Violence* (New York: Continuum, 1994), 148–149.

31. It may be that Roman Catholics will resonate most strongly with Rahner's theology of freedom for ultimate self-disposal, and be the most interested in the issue of how such a theology of freedom can respond adequately to the challenges of trauma theory. It is my hope, however, that this analysis of the dialogue between Rahner's theology of freedom and trauma theory will also be helpful for those Protestant Christians who also accord central importance to freedom for human fulfillment.

32. Anne Carr, "Theology and Experience in the Thought of Karl Rahner," *Journal of Religion* 53, 3 (July 1973): 359–376, and *The Theological Method of Karl Rahner* (Missoula, Mont.: Scholars Press, 1977).

33. Karl Rahner, *Foundations of Christian Faith: An Introduction to the Idea of Christianity* (New York: Crossroad, 1978), 25.

34. Karl Rahner, "The Current Relationship between Philosophy and Theology," in *Theological Investigations*, vol. 13 (New York: Seabury, 1975), 74; see also Rahner, "Reflections on Methodology in Theology," in *Theological Investigations*, vol. 2 (New York: Seabury, 1974), 74.

35. It is important to clarify from the outset that I do not focus here on the ultimate question of whether interpersonal harms can damn a person *qua passive victim*; the questions I pursue are not specifically the concern Outka raises about whether or not severe interpersonal harm can so distort a person's freedom that he or she ultimately chooses evil and is damned. Instead, I explore the credibility of the claim made by Jackson that interpersonal harm can render the exercise of freedom to love God and others inoperable; in this case, one cannot be damned for an evil choice since one's freedom is destroyed to such an extent that one is not morally culpable for an evil action.

36. Weil, *Waiting for God*, 119–120.

37. Ibid., 123.

38. See Diana Russell, "Incestuous Abuse of Females," in Kleber et al., 177.

CHAPTER 2

1. Rahner defines the term "existential" as a characteristic constitutive of human existence.

2. Rahner's account of how a person becomes a self-conscious knower will be very important when we consider how trauma affects one's self-awareness. For further explication of how spirit becomes self-aware in and through matter, see Karl Rahner,

Hearers of the Word, trans. Michael Richards (New York: Herder and Herder, 1969), and *Spirit in the World,* trans. William Dych (London: Sheed and Ward, 1968).

3. Rahner, *Foundations of Christian Faith,* 20.

4. Ibid., 20.

5. Ibid., 27.

6. Ibid., 29.

7. Ibid.

8. Ibid., 35.

9. Ibid., 39.

10. Karl Rahner, "Theology of Freedom," in *Theological Investigations,* vol. 6 (London: Darton, Longman and Todd, 1969), 183–184.

11. Karl Rahner, "Concerning the Relationship between Nature and Grace," in *Theological Investigations,* vol. 1 (London: Darton, Longman and Todd, 1961), 310.

12. Karl Rahner, "Grace," in *Encyclopedia of Theology: The Concise Sacramentum Mundi,* ed. Karl Rahner (London: Burns and Oates, 1975), 591.

13. Karl Rahner, "Reflections on the Unity of the Love of Neighbor and the Love of God," *Theological Investigations,* vol. 6, 245.

14. Rahner, *Foundations of Christian Faith,* 121.

15. Karl Rahner, "Religious Enthusiasm and the Experience of Grace," in *Theological Investigations,* vol. 16 (London: Darton, Longman and Todd, 1979), 40.

16. Rahner refers to this existential as supernatural in order to stress that God's self-offer is a gratuitous gift distinct from the other existentials that constitute human nature.

17. Rahner, *Foundations of Christian Faith,* 130.

18. Karl Rahner, "The Theological Concept of Concupiscentia," *Theological Investigations,* vol. 1, 377.

19. Karl Rahner, *Grace in Freedom* (New York: Herder and Herder, 1969), 209.

20. Rahner, "Reflections on the Experience of Grace," in *Theological Investigations,* vol. 3 (London: Darton, Longman and Todd, 1967), 86–90.

21. Rahner, "Grace," 594; Rahner, *Foundations of Christian Faith,* 125–129.

22. Rahner refers to God's self-offer as uncreated grace, since it is God in Godself that is offered rather than a created form of grace.

23. Rahner, "Grace," 587–595; Rahner, "Religious Enthusiasm and the Experience of Grace," 35–51.

24. Rahner, "Grace," 594.

25. Rahner, "Theology of Freedom," 184.

26. Rahner, *Grace in Freedom,* 212.

27. Ibid., 202.

28. Ibid., 211.

29. Rahner, *Foundations of Christian Faith,* 37.

30. Karl Rahner, "The 'Commandment' of Love in Relation to the Other Commandments," in *Theological Investigations,* vol. 5 (London: Darton, Longman, and Todd, 1966), 443.

31. Rahner, *Foundations of Christian Faith,* 104.

32. Rahner, "Theology of Freedom," 200.

33. Ibid., 101.

34. Ibid., 185.

35. Rahner, *Foundations of Christian Faith,* 98, emphasis in original.

36. Rahner, "Theology of Freedom," 187.

37. Ibid., 189–190.

38. See Rahner, "Reflections on the Experience of Grace" and "Theology of Freedom."

39. Karl Rahner, *The Love of Jesus and the Love of Neighbor* (New York: Crossroads, 1983), 71.

40. Ibid.

41. Rahner, "Reflections on the Unity of the Love of Neighbor and the Love of God," 242–243.

42. Rahner, "Theology of Freedom," 189.

43. Rahner, "Reflections on the Unity of the Love of Neighbor and the Love of God," 244.

44. Ibid., 241.

45. Ibid., 235.

46. See Rahner, *Foundations of Christian Faith,* 101. See also Rahner, "Theology of Freedom," 186.

47. Rahner, *Foundations of Christian Faith,* 97.

48. Ibid., 101–102.

49. Ibid., 101–102.

50. Ibid., 104.

51. Rahner, "Reflections on the Unity of the Love of Neighbor and the Love of God," 243.

52. For a more in-depth discussion, see Karl Rahner, "The Comfort of Time," *Theological Investigations,* vol. 3, 141–160.

53. Rahner, *Foundations of Christian Faith,* 96.

54. Rahner, "Theological Concept of Concupiscentia," 347–382. For Rahner, concupiscence is not necessarily a distorted desire or an evil.

55. Rahner, *Foundations of Christian Faith,* 104.

56. Rahner, "Why Does God Allow Us to Suffer?" in *Theological Investigations,* vol. 19 (London: Darton, Longman and Todd, 1983), 236.

57. Ibid., 243.

58. Rahner, *Foundations of Christian Faith,* 111.

59. Ibid., 109.

60. Ibid., 112.

61. Rahner, *Grace in Freedom,* 233.

62. Karl Rahner, "The Theology of Power," in *Theological Investigations,* vol. 4 (London: Darton, Longman and Todd, 1961), 391, emphasis mine.

63. Ibid., 405.

64. Rahner, "The Dignity and Freedom of Man," in *Theological Investigations,* vol. 2 (London: Darton, Longman and Todd, 1963), 242.

65. Ibid., 242.
66. Ibid., 250–251.
67. Ibid., 248.
68. Ibid., 249–250.
69. We will see in chapter 5 that Rahner briefly wavers twice in his writings about this issue. However, in the majority of his writings, he remains firmly committed to the belief that all persons who are capable of subjectivity inevitably say yes or no to God's self-offer.
70. When analyzing freedom in peripheral cases where persons lack reason, Rahner says: "We cannot go into the question whether and how this freedom can be accounted for in those peripheral cases where a person exists on a merely biological level, cases in which we do not recognize any concrete possibility of accounting for subjectivity, for example, the mentally handicapped who, at least by our normal standards, never seem to come to the use of reason. But we cannot understand something fundamental which is experienced at the center of existence in terms of such peripheral cases." See Rahner, *Foundations of Christian Faith*, 106.
71. Rahner, "Dignity and Freedom of Man," 242–243.
72. Since Rahner is focusing on freedom of ultimate self-disposal for or against God in this essay, it can be argued that his phrase "thing to be done" refers to the act of effecting a fundamental option.
73. Rahner, "Dignity and Freedom of Man," 248.
74. Rahner, "Comfort of Time," 151–152.
75. Rahner, *Foundations of Christian Faith*, 147.
76. Ibid., 116; Rahner, "Religious Enthusiasm and the Experience of Grace," 40.

CHAPTER 3

1. Unfortunately, due to the constraints of this chapter, I will not be able to attend adequately to the complex interrelationships between the effects of incestuous abuse and forms of social injustice—racism, classism, etc.
2. There is much debate whether the term "trauma victim" or "survivor" is more appropriate to use in reference to women who have been incestuously abused. The term "victim" most adequately conveys the long-term negative effects of child sexual abuse, and calls attention to the fact that a percentage of sexual abuse victims do not survive. The term "survivor," on the other hand, honors the ways the person has coped and survived the abuse. Since both emphases are important, I will use both terms throughout the book. I choose to concentrate on female incest survivors rather than both female and male survivors because the vast majority of incest survivors who have sought therapy and who have participated in studies have been female. Since there has been even greater resistance in acknowledging that males are victims of incest, it is not yet known how prevalent it is. Current data suggest that one in every three girls and one in every eight boys is sexually abused by an adult before the age of eighteen. Given the different socializations of females and males, it would be imprudent to generalize or assume that male incest survivors have

responded the same way as females. More research needs to be done on male survivors of incest before credible comparisons can be made. See David Finkelhor et al., eds., *Sourcebook on Child Sexual Abuse* (Newbury Park, Calif.: Sage, 1986).

3. J. Jeffrey Means, *Trauma and Evil: Healing the Wounded Soul* (Minneapolis: Fortress Press, 2000), 67.

4. Bessel van der Kolk et al., "History of Trauma in Psychiatry," in van der Kolk et al., *Traumatic Stress*, 56.

5. Diana E. H. Russell, *The Secret Trauma: Incest in the Lives of Girls and Women* (New York: Basic Books, 1986), 9–11.

6. Ibid., 10.

7. Ibid., 41.

8. In her study, Russell included several questions at the end of the interviews, asking if the participants had been unable to be honest about some issues. A few admitted that they were unable to be honest about child sexual abuse: Russell and Bolen, *The Epidemic of Rape and Child Sexual Abuse in the United States* (Thousand Oaks, Calif.: Sage, 2000), 212. See also Linda Williams, "Recall of Childhood Trauma: A Prospective Study of Women's Memories of Child Sexual Abuse," *Journal of Consulting and Clinical Psychology* 62 (1994): 1167–1176.

9. David Finkelhor et al., "Sexual Abuse in a National Survey of Adult Men and Women: Prevalence, Characteristics, and Risk Factors," *Child Abuse and Neglect* 14, 1 (1990): 19–28.

10. These factors have been shown to contribute to findings of lower prevalence rates than studies where interviews are conducted in person, last longer, and include more questions about child sexual abuse. See Russell and Bolen, *Epidemic of Rape.*

11. P. Schene, "Child Abuse and Neglect Policy, History, Models, and Future Directions," in *The APSAC Handbook of Child Maltreatment*, ed. J. Briere et al. (Thousand Oaks, Calif.: Sage, 1996), 386.

12. Bessel van der Kolk et al., "Dissociation and Information Processing in Posttraumatic Stress Disorder," in van der Kolk et al., *Traumatic Stress*, 303.

13. Judith Herman, *Trauma and Recovery* (New York: Basic Books, 1992), 107.

14. Ibid., 52.

15. Ibid., 96.

16. Ibid., 101.

17. Ibid., 102; J. Chu and D. Dill, "Dissociative Symptoms in Relation to Child Physical and Sexual Abuse," *American Journal of Psychiatry* 147 (1990): 887–892.

18. Herman, *Trauma and Recovery*, 103.

19. Ibid.

20. Bessel van der Kolk, "Trauma and Memory," in van der Kolk et al., *Traumatic Stress*, 286.

21. Lenore Terr, "Childhood Traumas: An Outline and Overview," *American Journal of Psychiatry* 148, 1 (1991): 10–20.

22. Elizabeth Waites, *Trauma and Survival: Post-traumatic and Dissociative Disorders in Women* (New York: Norton, 1993), 100.

23. Judith Herman, "Complex PTSD: A Syndrome in Survivors of Prolonged and Repeated Trauma," in *Psychotraumatology*, ed. George Everly and Jeffrey Lating (New York: Plenum Press, 1995), 87–102.

24. Herman, *Trauma and Recovery*, 108.

25. Van der Kolk and McFarlane, "Black Hole of Trauma," 9.

26. Herman, *Trauma and Recovery*, 108–109.

27. It is inaccurate to depict this response as consciously chosen; as van der Kolk and McFarlane note, "Hyperarousal depletes both the biological and psychological resources needed to experience a variety of emotions" ("Black Hole of Trauma," 12). Although the neurobiological basis for emotional numbing is complex and presently unclear, researchers believe that there are long-term changes in the central nervous system in response to chronic, repeated trauma. See Bessel van der Kolk, "The Body Keeps the Score: Approaches to the Psychobiology of Posttraumatic Stress Disorder," in van der Kolk et al., *Traumatic Stress*, 214–241; Bessel van der Kolk et al., "A General Approach to Treatment of Posttraumatic Stress Disorder," in van der Kolk et al., *Traumatic Stress*, 417–440.

28. Lisa M. Najavits, *Seeking Safety: A Treatment Manual for PTSD and Substance Abuse* (New York: Guilford Press, 2002), and Lisa M. Najavits, "Assessment of Trauma, PTSD, and Substance Use Disorder: A Practical Guide," in *Assessing Psychological Trauma and PTSD*, ed. John P. Wilson and Terence M. Keane (New York: Guilford Press, 2004), 466–491.

29. Waites, *Trauma and Survival*, 116.

30. Herman, *Trauma and Recovery*, 109. These destructive ways of regulating emotions are often established in children before adolescence and often increase in severity during adolescence.

31. Ibid., 41.

32. Linda J. Koenig, ed., *From Child Sexual Abuse to Adult Sexual Risk: Trauma, Revictimization, and Intervention* (Washington, D.C.: American Psychological Association, 2004); Herman, *Trauma and Recovery*, 109–113; Susan Turell and Mary Armsworth, "Differentiating Incest Survivors Who Self-Mutilate," *Child Abuse and Neglect* 24, 2 (2000): 237–249.

33. J. R. Davidson et al., "The Association of Sexual Assault and Attempted Suicide Within the Community," *Archives of General Psychiatry* 53 (1996): 550–555; D. Peters and L. Range, "Childhood Sexual Abuse and Current Suicidality in College Women and Men, *Child Abuse and Neglect* 19, 3 (1995): 335–341; S. Bryant and L. Range, "Suicidality in College Women Who Were Sexually and Physically Abused and Physically Punished by Parents," *Violence and Victims* 10, 3 (1995): 195–201; S. Stepakoff, "Effects of Sexual Victimization on Suicidal Ideation and Behavior in U.S. College Women," *Suicide and Life-Threatening Behavior* 28, 1 (1998): 107–126.

34. Of course, many other incest victims-survivors attempt to protect younger siblings from being abused, even when this results in great cost to themselves. See Herman, *Trauma and Recovery*, 104.

35. Ibid., 112; E. H. Carmen, P. P. Rieker, and T. Mills, "Victims of Violence and Psychiatric Illness," *American Journal of Psychiatry* 141 (1984): 378–383.

36. Russell, *Secret Trauma*, 158.

37. Van der Kolk, "The Complexity of Adaptation to Trauma," in van der Kolk et al., *Traumatic Stress*, 200. See D. Finkelhor and A. Browne, "The Traumatic Impact of Child Sexual Abuse: A Conceptualization," *American Journal of Orthopsychiatry* 55 (1984): 530–541; M. Silbert and A. Pines, "Sexual Child Abuse as an Antecedent to Prostitution," *Bulletin of the Menninger Clinic* 45 (1981): 428–438.

38. Herman, *Trauma and Recovery*, 112.

39. Barbara Krahé, "Child Sexual Abuse and Revictimization in Adolescence and Adulthood," in *Post-traumatic Stress Theory*, ed. Jon Harvey and Brian Pauwels (Philadelphia: Brunner/Mazel, 2000), 52.

40. Herman, "Complex PTSD," 94–95.

41. Seymour Epstein, "Cognitive-Experiential Self Theory: Implications for Developmental Psychology," *Self Processes and Development* 23 (1991): 78–124; Susan Harter, "The Effects of Child Abuse on the Self-System," in *Multiple Victimization of Children: Conceptual, Developmental, Research, and Treatment Issues*, ed. B. B. Robbie Rossman and Mindy S. Rosenberg (New York: Haworth Maltreatment and Trauma Press, 1998), 147–170; Harter, *The Construction of the Self* (New York: Guilford Press, 1999), 268–282; Jon Allen, *Coping with Trauma: A Guide to Understanding* (Washington, D.C.: American Psychiatric Press, 1995), 128–140.

42. Allen, *Coping with Trauma*, 128; Harter, "Effects of Child Abuse," 159–160.

43. Allen, *Coping with Trauma*, 128.

44. Harter, "Effects of Child Abuse," 149.

45. It is important to note that sexually abused children are also vulnerable to being emotionally and physically abused or neglected as well. See Allen, *Coping with Trauma*, 132.

46. Various neurological studies are suggesting that changes in brain activity cause an inability to interpret states as emotions and articulate them in words. See van der Kolk, "Body Keeps the Score," 231–233.

47. Dante Cicchetti, "How Research on Child Maltreatment Has Informed the Study of Child Development: Perspectives from Developmental Psychology," in *Child Maltreatment: Theory and Research on the Causes and Consequences of Child Abuse and Neglect*, ed. D. Cicchetti and V. Carlson (New York: Cambridge University Press, 1989), 377–431; D. Cicchetti et al., "The Emergence of the Self in Atypical Populations," in *The Self in Transition: Infancy to Childhood*, ed. D. Cicchetti and M. Beeghley (Chicago: University of Chicago Press, 1990), 309–344.

48. Daniel Stern, *The Interpersonal World of the Infant: A View from Psychoanalysis and Development Psychology* (New York: Basic Books, 1985), 71.

49. Allen, *Coping with Trauma*, 130–135.

50. Herman, *Trauma and Recovery*, 108.

51. Stern, *Interpersonal World of the Infant*, 71.

52. John Briere, *Child Abuse Trauma: Theory and Treatment of the Lasting Effects* (Newbury Park, Calif.: Sage, 1992); A. Browne and D. Finkelhor, "Impact of Child Sexual Abuse: A Review of the Research," *Psychological Bulletin* 99 (1986): 66–77;

K. Kendall-Tackett et al., "Impact of Sexual Abuse on Children: A Review and Synthesis of Recent Empirical Studies," *Psychological Bulletin* 113 (1993): 164–180.

53. Harter, "Effects of Child Abuse," 149–150.

54. Herman, *Trauma and Recovery*, 105.

55. Ibid.

56. Catherine Cameron, *Resolving Childhood Trauma* (London: Sage, 2000), 151.

57. Herman, *Trauma and Recovery*, 114.

58. Since the terms "autonomy" and "agency" are used interchangeably throughout the trauma psychological literature, I will also do so.

59. Harter, "Effects of Child Abuse," 156; James Childress, *Who Should Decide?* (Oxford: Oxford University Press, 1982), 61.

60. Diana T. Meyers, *Self, Society, and Personal Choice* (New York: Columbia University Press, 1989), 52.

61. Judith Herman, *Father-Daughter Incest* (Cambridge, Mass.: Harvard University Press, 1981), 125.

62. Leslie Beth Berger, *Incest, Work and Women* (Springfield, Ill.: Charles C. Thomas, 1998), 29.

63. Herman, *Trauma and Recovery*, 112.

64. Russell, *Secret Trauma*, 201.

65. Berger, *Incest, Work and Women*, 51–66.

66. Ibid., 15.

67. Ibid., 30.

68. Ronnie Janoff-Bulman, *Shattered Assumptions* (New York: Free Press, 1992). Lenore Terr has also found that a central effect of trauma on children is a foreshortened sense of the future. See Terr, "Childhood Traumas: An Outline and Overview," *American Journal of Psychiatry* 148, 1 (1991): 10–20.

69. Berger, *Incest, Work and Women*, 14–15.

70. Ibid., 74–78.

71. Some research studies have found that 95 percent of patients with multiple personality disorders had been severely sexually and/or physically abused as children. See M. M. Coons, "Child Abuse and Multiple Personality Disorder: Review of the Literature and Suggestions for Treatment," *Child Abuse and Neglect* 10, 4 (1986): 455–462.

72. Herman, *Trauma and Recovery*, 194. See also Coffey, *Unspeakable Truths and Happy Endings.*

73. Herman, *Trauma and Recovery*, 111.

74. Krahé, "Child Sexual Abuse and Revictimization in Adolescence and Adulthood," 49–66.

75. Finkelhor and Browne, "Traumatic Impact of Child Sexual Abuse," 530–541.

76. Elaine Westerlund, *Women's Sexuality after Childhood Incest* (New York: Norton, 1992), 56–57.

77. Victoria Banyard, "The Impact of Childhood Sexual Abuse and Family Functioning on Four Dimensions of Women's Later Parenting," *Child Abuse and Neglect* 21, 11 (1997): 1095–1107; Tamar Cohen, "Motherhood Among Incest Survivors,"

Child Abuse and Neglect 19, 12 (2000): 1423–1429; Anne Douglas, "Reported Anxieties Concerning Intimate Parenting in Women Sexually Abused as Children," *Child Abuse and Neglect* 24, 3 (2000): 425–434; Ayelet Ruscio, "Predicting the Child-Rearing Practices of Mothers Sexually Abused in Childhood," *Child Abuse and Neglect* 25, 3 (2001): 369–387; Westerlund, *Women's Sexuality after Childhood Incest*; Pamela M. Cole et al., "Parenting Difficulties: Adult Survivors of Father-Daughter Incest," *Child Abuse and Neglect* 16, 2 (1992): 39–49.

78. Mary Armsworth and Karin Stronck, "Intergenerational Effects of Incest on Parenting: Skills, Abilities, and Attitudes," *Journal of Counseling & Development* 77, 3 (1999): 303–315.

79. Ibid.

80. Douglas, "Reported Anxieties Concerning Intimate Parenting," 425.

81. C. Kreklewetz and C. Piotrowski, "Incest Survivor Mothers: Protecting the Next Generation," *Child Abuse and Neglect* 22, 12 (1998): 1305–1312; Armsworth, "Intergenerational Effects of Incest."

82. S. Zuravin et al., "The Intergenerational Cycle of Child Maltreatment: Continuity vs. Discontinuity," *Journal of Interpersonal Violence* 11, 3 (1996): 15–34; R. Oates et al., "Prior Sexual Abuse in Mothers of Sexually Abused Children," *Child Abuse and Neglect* 22, 11 (1998): 1113–1118.

83. Donna Kane et al., "Perception of God by Survivors of Childhood Sexual Abuse: An Exploratory Study in an Underresearched Area," *Journal of Psychology and Theology* 21 (1993): 228–237; Manlowe, *Faith Born of Seduction;* John Lemoncelli and Andrew Carey, "The Psychospiritual Dynamics of Adult Survivors of Abuse," *Counseling and Values* 40 (1996): 175–185; Stephen Rossetti, "The Impact of Child Sexual Abuse on Attitudes toward God and the Catholic Church," *Child Abuse and Neglect* 19, 12 (1995): 1469–1481; William Justice and Warren Lambert, "A Comparative Study of the Language People Use to Describe the Personalities of God and Their Earthly Parents," *Journal of Pastoral Care* 40, 2 (1986): 166–172. One study, conducted by Shelley Todd was an exception, reporting no significant difference in the God-concept among incest victims and nonabused women. While she found that incest abuse victims expressed great ambivalence concerning God, she did not find a distinct pattern of difference in God-concepts of survivors and nonabused women. This might be due to the fact that this was a voluntary study, and attracted only those survivors who were already interested in and open to spirituality issues and a relationship with God. Shelley Todd, "An Exploration of the Concept of God Espoused by Female Adult Survivors of Sexual Abuse," Ph.D. diss., New Orleans Baptist Theological Seminary, 1991.

84. Lemoncelli, "Psychospiritual Dynamics of Adult Survivors of Abuse," 175–185; Manlowe, *Faith Born of Seduction*, 79–92; Mary Crist Brown, *Free to Believe: Liberating Images of God for Women* (Cleveland: Pilgrim Press, 2000). Russell, *Secret Trauma*, 119–122.

85. Brown, *Free to Believe*, 61.

86. Lemoncelli, "Psychospiritual Dynamics of Adult Survivors of Abuse," 175–185.

87. Christine Courtois, *Healing the Incest Wound: Adult Survivors in Therapy* (New York: Norton, 1988), 202.

88. Justice and Lambert, "A Comparative Study of the Language People Use," 237.

89. Terese Hall, "Spiritual Effects of Childhood Sexual Abuse in Adult Christian Women," *Journal of Psychology and Theology* 23 (1995): 129–134.

90. Manlowe, *Faith Born of Seduction*, 83.

91. Justice and Lambert, "A Comparative Study of the Language People Use," 166–172; Lemoncelli, "Psychospiritual Dynamics of Adult Survivors of Abuse," 175–185.

92. P. Benson and B. Spilka, "God Image as a Function of Self-Esteem and Locus of Control," *Journal for the Scientific Study of Religion* 12 (1973): 297–310; M. Chartier and L. Goehner, "A Study of the Relationship of Parent-Adolescent Communication, Self-Esteem, and God Image," *Journal of Psychology and Theology* 4 (1976): 227–232; J. Buri, "Psychoanalytic Bases for One's Image of God: Fact or Artifact?" paper presented at the 62nd annual meeting of the Midwestern Psychological Association, Chicago, May 1990; J. Buri and R. Mueller, "Conceptions of Parents, Conceptions of Self, and Conceptions of God," paper presented at the annual convention of the American Psychological Association, New York, May 1987.

93. Lilliam Torre, "Predictors of the Concept of God in a Sample of Adult Survivors of Father-Daughter Incest" (Ph.D. diss., University of Miami, 1993).

CHAPTER 4

1. Claudia Card, *The Unnatural Lottery: Character and Moral Luck* (Philadelphia: Temple University Press, 1996), 4. See also Claudia Card, "Oppression and Resistance: Frye's Politics of Reality," *Hypatia* 1, 1 (April 1986): 149–166.

2. See, for instance, Sheila Davaney, "Continuing the Story, but Departing the Text: A Historicist Interpretation of Feminist Norms in Theology," in *Horizons in Feminist Theology: Identity, Tradition, and Norms*, ed. Rebecca S. Chopp and Sheila Davaney (Minneapolis: Fortress Press, 1997), 198–214, 257–258; Sheila Davaney, "The Limits of the Appeal to Women's Experience," in *Shaping New Vision*, ed. Clarissa Atkinson et al. (Ann Arbor, Mich.: VMI Research Press, 1987), 31–49; Mary McClintock Fulkerson, "Changing the Subject: Feminist Theology and Discourse," *Literature and Theology* 10 (June 1996): 131–147.

3. Judith Butler, "Contingent Foundations," in *Feminist Contentions: A Philosophical Exchange*, ed. Seyla Benhabib et al. (New York: Routledge, 1995), 46.

4. Ibid., 137.

5. Chris Weedon, *Feminist Practice and Poststructuralist Theory* (Oxford: Blackwell, 1987), 32.

6. Judith Butler, *Gender Trouble: Feminism and the Subversion of Identity* (New York: Routledge, 1990) 145.

7. Ibid., 10.

8. Judith Butler, "Performing Acts and Gender Constitution: An Essay in Phenomenology and Feminist Theory," in *Performing Feminisms: Feminist Critical Theory and Theatre*, ed. Sue Ellen Case (Baltimore: John Hopkins University Press, 1990), 277.

9. Butler, *Gender Trouble,* 25.

10. Ibid., 142.

11. Butler, "For a Careful Reading," 134–136.

12. Butler, *Gender Trouble,* 136.

13. Judith Butler, "Variations on Sex and Gender," in *Feminism as Critique: Essays on the Politics of Gender in Late Capitalist Societies,* ed. Seyla Benhabib and Drucilla Cornell (Cambridge: Polity, 1987), 134.

14. Judith Butler, *Bodies That Matter: On the Discursive Limits of "Sex"* (New York: Routledge, 1993), x.

15. Ibid., xi.

16. Ibid., 11.

17. Ibid., 10.

18. Jacinta Kerins, "The Matter at Hand: Butler, Ontology, and the Natural Sciences," *Australian Feminist Studies* 14, 29 (1999), 91–104.

19. Butler, *Gender Trouble,* 17.

20. Ibid., 16.

21. Ibid., 143.

22. Butler, "Contingent Foundations," 47.

23. Ibid., 46–47.

24. Ibid., 46.

25. Butler, *Bodies That Matter,* 220.

26. Butler, *Gender Trouble,* 135.

27. Butler, "Contingent Foundations," 47.

28. Lise Nelson, "Bodies (and Spaces) Do Matter: The Limits of Performativity," *Gender, Place and Culture* 6 (1999): 331–354.

29. Butler, *Gender Trouble,* 145.

30. Butler, "For a Careful Reading," 135.

31. Ibid., 134.

32. Ibid.

33. For more discussion, see Veronica Vasterling, "Butler's Sophisticated Constructivism: A Critical Assessment," *Hypatia* 14, 3 (1999): 17–38; Nelson, "Bodies (and Spaces) Do Matter," 331–354. See especially Butler, *Gender Trouble,* 28, 145; *Bodies That Matter,* 118, 125, 227, 241.

34. Butler, "Contingent Foundations," 42.

35. Vasterling, "Butler's Sophisticated Constructivism," 17–38; Nelson, "Bodies (and Spaces) Do Matter," 331–354.

36. Butler, *The Psychic Life of Power: Theories in Subjection* (Stanford, Calif.: Stanford University Press, 1997), 18.

37. Ibid., 2, 5, 86–87.

38. Ibid., 3.

39. Ibid., 9.

40. Ibid., 15.

41. It is beyond the scope of this chapter to analyze in greater depth Butler's analysis of the formation of the psyche. Although she argues that the psyche is

"precisely what exceeds the imprisoning effects of the discursive demand to inhabit a coherent identity," her account of how subjects become passionately attached to subjection, which further reifies their identities, seems to undermine the subversive potential of the psyche (ibid., 86).

42. Catherine Mills, "Efficacy and Vulnerability: Judith Butler on Reiteration and Resistance," *Australian Feminist Studies* 15, 32 (2000), 271–277.

43. Butler, *Psychic Life of Power*, 6–8.

44. Butler, "Contingent Foundations," 42.

45. Butler, *Gender Trouble*, 145.

46. Trauma research findings that supportive relations are necessary in the process of developing agency and making constructive changes may provide important insights for Butler's project of theorizing what makes motivation for resistance possible; it would seem the existence of supportive others is a significant factor in inspiring social resistance—a fact Butler does not appear to explore sufficiently in her work.

47. Herman, *Trauma and Recovery*; van der Kolk et al., *Traumatic Stress*.

48. Jane Flax, *Thinking Fragments: Psychoanalysis, Feminism and Postmodernism in the Contemporary West* (Berkeley: University of California Press, 1990), 218.

49. Butler, *Bodies That Matter*, 31.

50. Judith Herman, *Trauma and Recovery*; van der Kolk et al., *Traumatic Stress*; Russell, *Secret Trauma*.

51. Leslie Young, "Sexual Abuse and the Problem of Embodiment," *Child Abuse and Neglect* 16, 1 (1992), 89–100.

52. Ibid.

53. By emphasizing the point that bodily responses to sexual violence limit the scope of credible discourses about bodily well-being, I am not suggesting that children's experiences of sexual abuse and traumatization are not significantly shaped by their social discourses; I am merely arguing that, in addition to discourses, the biological and physiological makeup of children's bodies also affects their developing psyche and developing subjectivity.

54. Butler, *Bodies That Matter*, 29.

55. Ibid. See also Judith Butler, Ernesto Laclau, and Slavoj Žižek, *Contingency, Hegemony, Universality: Contemporary Dialogues on the Left* (London: Versa: 2000).

56. An alarming number of Internet websites are authored by parents and adults who defend sexual practices with children.

57. Although the majority of persons in society may condemn child sexual abuse, the high incidence of sexual abuse and societal acceptance of all discourses that foster exploitation of women and children demonstrate that preventing child sexual abuse is not a high priority in our society.

58. Meyers, *Self, Society, and Personal Choice*, 26.

59. Ibid., 27–30.

60. Ibid.

61. Ibid., 40.

62. Ibid., 19.

63. Ibid., 20.

64. Ibid.

65. Diana T. Meyers, "Personal Autonomy or the Deconstructed Subject? A Reply to Heckman," *Hypatia* 7, 1 (Winter 1992): 125.

66. Meyers, *Self, Society, and Personal Choice*, 76.

67. Ibid., 55.

68. Ibid., 20.

69. Ibid., 133–171.

70. Ibid., 215.

71. Rahner frequently argues that he presumes that persons with reason possess freedom to effect a fundamental option and ultimately determine who they will become. See, for instance, Rahner, *Foundations of Christian Faith*, 106; Rahner, *Love of Jesus and the Love of Neighbor*, 101–102.

72. Meyers, *Self, Society, and Personal Choice*, xi.

73. I interviewed "Lauren" during a series of interviews that totaled fifteen hours. The interviews were conducted during a two-year period (from December 2002 to February 2003).

74. Meyers, *Self, Society, and Personal Choice*, 61. It is difficult to understand how Meyers's account of persons superseding cultural norms escapes the quest of transcending socialization—the main critique she mounts against free will accounts of autonomy.

75. For Meyers, a heteronomous desire that undermines the process of acquiring autonomy skills constitutes an unhealthy desire.

76. For further discussion of the need for substantive criteria in philosophical accounts of autonomy see Paul Benson, "Free Agency and Self-Worth," *Journal of Philosophy* 91 (1994): 650–668; Robin Dillon, "Toward a Feminist Conception of Self-Respect," *Hypatia* 7 (Winter 1992): 52–69, and "Self-Respect: Moral, Emotional, Political," *Ethics* 107 (January 1997): 226–249.

CHAPTER 5

1. Rahner, *Foundations of Christian Faith*, 101–102.

2. Quotation: Rahner, *On the Theology of Death* (New York: Herder and Herder, 1961), 94.

3. Rahner, *Foundations of Christian Faith*, 39.

4. Michael DiPaolo, *The Impact of Multiple Childhood Trauma on Homeless Runaway Adolescents* (New York: Garland, 1999).

5. Rahner, "Religious Enthusiasm and the Experience of Grace," 40; Rahner, "Grace," 594; Rahner, *Foundations of Christian Faith*, 125–129.

6. Rahner, *Foundations of Christian Faith*, 131.

7. Ibid., 151, emphasis mine.

8. Ibid., 52, 151–152.

9. Rahner, "Reflections on the Experience of Grace," 87.

10. Ibid., 89.

11. Rahner, *Love of Jesus and the Love of Neighbor,* 17.

12. Quotations: Rahner, "Religious Feeling Inside and Outside the Church," in *Theological Investigations,* vol. 17 (New York: Crossroad, 1981), 236.

13. Rahner, "Reflections on the Experience of Grace," 87.

14. Quotation: ibid., 89.

15. I am not suggesting that traumatized persons are free from the existential of sin; I am merely arguing that the struggle against sinful egoism does not adequately explain their struggles with vitiated agency and relating constructively to others.

16. As demonstrated by previously quoted passages, Rahner has explicitly denied that external threats have the power to incapacitate entirely a person's ability to respond to God's grace and effect a positive fundamental option.

17. Rahner, "Current Relationship between Philosophy and Theology," 74.

18. By "coherency with the Christian tradition" I mean here the strand of the Christian tradition that affirms a role for human freedom in response to God's grace.

19. Rahner, *Foundations of Christian Faith,* 37.

20. Rahner, "Theology of Freedom," 190.

21. Means, *Trauma and Evil.*

22. Rahner, *Foundations of Christian Faith,* 403.

23. Karl Rahner, *Meditations of Freedom and the Spirit* (New York: Seabury Press, 1978), 38, emphasis mine.

24. Karl Rahner, "Christian Dying," in *Theological Investigations,* vol. 18 (New York: Crossroad, 1983), 237.

25. Rahner explicitly mentions developmentally disabled persons, children who died before the age of reason, and the unborn. See Rahner, *Foundations of Christian Faith*; Rahner, *Love of Jesus and the Love of Neighbor,* 101–102.

26. Rahner, "Theology of Freedom," 233.

27. Rahner, *Love of Jesus and the Love of Neighbor,* 101–102.

28. Rahner, "Comfort of Time," 151–152.

29. Rahner, *Foundations of Christian Faith,* 26.

30. Ibid., 147.

31. Ibid., 30–31.

32. Ibid., 219.

33. Karl Rahner, "The Liberty of the Sick, Theologically Considered," in *Theological Investigations,* vol. 17, 107.

34. Karl Rahner, *I Remember* (New York: Crossroad, 1985), 104–105.

35. I develop this point in greater detail below.

36. Karl Rahner, "Purgatory," in *Theological Investigations,* vol. 19 (New York: Crossroad, 1983), 191.

37. Ibid.

38. Rahner, *Theology of Pastoral Action* (New York: Herder and Herder, 1968), 47.

39. Karl Rahner, *The Church and the Sacraments* (New York: Herder and Herder, 1963), 22.

40. Rahner, "The Church's Commission to Bring Salvation and the Humanization of the World," in *Theological Investigations*, vol. 14 (New York: Seabury Press, 1976), 295–313. See also Rahner, *Theology of Pastoral Action*.

41. Karl Rahner, "On the Theology of the Council," in *Theological Investigations*, vol. 5, 252.

42. Rahner, "Church's Commission," 68.

43. Ibid., 41.

44. Ibid., 69.

45. Ibid., 67.

46. Given Rahner's theology of anonymous Christians and his conviction about the universality of grace, it is important to underscore that the social mediation of grace also occurs outside official membership in the institutional church.

47. Rahner generally emphasizes only the former sense of intersubjectivity in his writings.

CHAPTER 6

1. Mari West Zimmerman, *Take and Make Holy: Honoring the Sacred in the Healing Journey of Abuse Survivors* (Chicago: Liturgy Training, 1995).

2. Rahner, *Foundations of Christian Faith*, 344–345.

3. Marcia Sheinberg and Peter Fraenkel, *The Relational Trauma of Incest* (New York: Guilford Press, 2001).

4. Ibid.

5. Rahner, *Foundations of Christian Faith*, 111.

6. Ibid., 147.

7. Herman, *Trauma and Recovery*.

8. *The Book of Discipline of the United Methodist Church* (Nashville, Tenn.: United Methodist Publishing House, 1996); *Psalter Hymnal: Doctrinal Standards and Liturgy of the Christian Reformed Church* (Grand Rapids, Mich.: Publication Committee of the Christian Reformed Church, 1959); *Selected Theological Statements of the Presbyterian Church* (Louisville, Ky.: Presbyterian Church (USA) Office of Theology and Worship, 1998); *Catechism of the Catholic Church*, 2nd ed. (Washington, D.C.: United States Catholic Conference, 2000).

9. National Review Board for the Protection of Children and Young People, *A Report on the Crisis in the Catholic Church in the United States* (Washington, D.C.: United States Conference of Catholic Bishops, 2004); John Jay College of Criminal Justice, *The Nature and Scope of the Problem of Sexual Abuse of Minors by Catholic Priests and Deacons in the United States* (Washington, D.C.: United States Conference of Catholic Bishops, 2004); Carolyn Holderread Heggen, *Sexual Abuse in Christian Homes and Churches* (Scottdale, Pa.: Herald Press, 1993), 14; Mary Potter Engel, "Evil, Sin, and Violation of the Vulnerable," in *Lift Every Voice: Constructing Christian Theology from the Underside*, ed. Mary Potter Engel (Maryknoll, N.Y.: Orbis Books, 1998), 159–172; Marie M. Fortune, ed., *Violence in the Family: A Workshop*

Curriculum for Clergy and Other Helpers (Cleveland: Pilgrim Press, 1991); Marie M. Fortune, *Sexual Violence: The Unmentionable Sin* (Cleveland: Pilgrim Press, 1983).

10. Hilary Cashman, *Christianity and Child Sexual Abuse* (London: Society for Promoting Christian Knowledge, 1993), 79–83; Christine E. Gudorf, *Victimization: Examining Christian Complacency*, 90–94.

11. Cashman, *Christianity and Child Sexual Abuse*, 11.

12. Marie Fortune, "Forgiveness: The Last Step," in *Violence Against Women and Children: A Christian Theological Sourcebook*, ed. Carol Adams and Marie Fortune (New York: Continuum, 1995), 201.

13. National Review Board for the Protection of Children and Young People, *A Report on the Crisis in the Catholic Church in the United States*, 106–107.

14. Ibid.

15. Mary Potter Engel, "Historical Theology and Violence Against Women," in Adams and Fortune, *Violence Against Women and Children*, 242–261; Mary Potter Engel, "Historical Theology and Violence Against Women: Unearthing Popular Tradition of Just Battery," in *Revisioning the Past*, ed. Mary Potter Engel and Walter Wyman (Minneapolis: Augsburg Fortress, 1992), 55; Rosemary Radford Ruether, "The Western Religious Tradition and Violence Against Women in the Home," in *Christianity, Patriarchy, and Abuse: A Feminist Critique*, ed. Joanne Carlson Brown and Carole R. Bohn (New York: Pilgrim Press, 1989), 31; Joy Bussert, *Battered Women: From a Theology of Suffering to an Ethic of Empowerment* (New York: Lutheran Church in America, 1986).

16. Hosea 2:19; Ezekiel 16 and 23; Jeremiah 1–3, 13.

17. Renita J. Weems, *Battered Love: Marriage, Sex, and Violence in the Hebrew Prophets* (Minneapolis: Fortress Press, 1995).

18. Judges 19:2, 11:29–40; Genesis 19:8.

19. See, for example, Ephesians 5:22–23; 1 Corinthians 11:7–9; 1 Corinthians 14:34–35; 1 Timothy 2:11–15.

20. During two years (1995–97) of counseling and teaching male batterers at Project to End Abuse through Counseling and Education (PEACE), I frequently encountered Christian men who justified their violence by appealing to scripture.

21. Marjorie Procter-Smith, "Reorganizing Victimization," in Adams and Fortune, *Violence Against Women and Children*, 431; Joy Bussert, *Battered Women from a Theology of Suffering to an Ethic of Empowerment* (New York: Division for Mission in North America, Lutheran Church in America, 1986).

22. Rita Brock and Joanne Carlson Brown, "For God So Loved the World?" in Adams and Fortune, *Violence Against Women and Children*, 36–59; Rita Brock, *Journeys by Heart: A Christology of Erotic Power* (New York: Crossroad, 1988).

23. Brock, *Journeys by Heart*; Heggen, *Sexual Abuse in Christian Homes and Churches*, 94–96; Annie Imbens, *Christianity and Incest* (Minneapolis: Fortress Press, 1992), 238–240.

24. Steven Tracy, "Sexual Abuse and Forgiveness," *Journal of Psychology and Theology* 27, 3 (1999): 219–229, Heggen, *Sexual Abuse in Christian Homes and Chur-*

ches; Pamela Cooper-White, *The Cry of Tamar: Violence Against Women and the Church's Response* (Philadelphia: Fortress, 1995).

25. Bill Gothard, *Supplementary Alumni Book, Research in Principles of Life*, vol. 5 (Oak Park, Ill.: Institute in Basic Youth Conflicts, 1979), 10. For further discussion, see Bussert, *Battered Women*, 64.

26. Fortune, "Forgiveness," 201–206; Manlowe, *Faith Born of Seduction*, 65–66; Heggen, *Sexual Abuse in Christian Homes and Churches*, 96–97, 121–132; Imbens, *Christianity and Incest*, 235–237; Keree Casey, "Surviving Abuse: Shame, Anger, Forgiveness," *Pastoral Psychology* 46, 4 (March 1998): 223–231.

27. See the feminist biblical scholars and theologians cited in earlier notes. In addition, certain theological work on agape has emphasized that love for neighbor precludes exploitation or victimization by that neighbor. See Gene Outka, *Agape: An Ethical Analysis* (New Haven, Conn.: Yale University Press, 1972), particularly his discussion against issuing the neighbor a blank check: 21–24, 209, 275–277.

28. Manlowe, *Faith Born of Seduction;* Imbens, *Christianity and Incest.*

29. Nancy Poling, ed., *Victim to Survivor: Women Recovering from Sexual Abuse* (Cleveland: United Church Press, 1999). See literature from the Faith Trust Institute.

30. National Review Board for the Protection of Children and Young People, *A Report on the Crisis in the Catholic Church in the United States*, 2004.

31. Kathryn Flynn, *The Sexual Abuse of Women by Members of the Clergy* (Jefferson, N.C.: McFarland & Company, 2003); Paul Isley, "Child Sexual Abuse and the Catholic Church: An Historical and Contemporary Review," *Pastoral Psychology* 45, 4 (1997): 277–299; Brian F. Linnane, "Celibacy and Sexual Malpractice: Dimensions of Power and Powerlessness in Patriarchal Society," in *Theology and the New Histories*, ed. Gary Macy (Maryknoll, N.Y.: Orbis, 1999), 227–244; Marie M. Fortune, *Is Nothing Sacred? When Sex Invades the Pastoral Relationship* (San Francisco: Harper and Row, 1989); Marie M. Fortune, "Responding to Clergy Sexual Abuse: An Interview," *Witness* 75 (December 1992): 15–19; John C. Gonsiorek, ed., *Breach of Trust: Sexual Exploitation by Health Care Professionals and Clergy* (Thousand Oaks, Calif.: Sage, 1995); Anson D. Shupe, ed., *Wolves Within the Fold* (New Brunswick, N.J.: Rutgers University Press, 1998); Stephen Rossetti, *Tragic Grace: The Catholic Church and Child Sexual Abuse* (Collegeville, Minn.: Liturgical Press, 1996); Richard John Neuhaus, "When Shepherds Go Astray," *First Things* 29 (1993) 55–58; Donald Clark, "Sexual Abuse in the Church: The Law Steps In," *The Christian Century* 110, 12 (April 14, 1993) 396–398. See also the website for the Faith Trust Institute.

32. Donald Cozzens, *Sacred Silence: Denial and the Crisis in the Church* (Collegeville, Minn.: Liturgical Press, 2004); Fortune, *Is Nothing Sacred?*; G. Lloyd Rediger, *Ministry and Sexuality* (Minneapolis: Fortress Press, 1990); Gonsiorek, *Breach of Trust*; Shupe, *Wolves Within the Fold.*

33. Office of Child and Youth Protection, *Report on the Implementation of the Charter for the Protection of Children and Young People* (Washington D.C.: United States Conference of Catholic Bishops, 2005).

34. See the websites for the Faith Trust Institute and for the Interfaith Sexual Trauma Institute.

35. Fortune, "Forgiveness," 202.

36. For instance, Christian communities can create a scholarship fund to help survivors pursue medical treatment and/or therapy.

37. Marie Fortune, "Justice Making in the Aftermath of Woman Battering," in Fortune, *Violence in the Family*, 179–190.

38. Flora Keshgegian, *Redeeming Memories* (Nashville, Tenn.: Abingdon Press, 2000), 43.

39. Ibid., 231.

40. Joanne Feldmeth and Midge Finley, *We Weep for Ourselves and for Our Children* (San Francisco: HarperSanFrancisco, 1990), 143.

41. While certain interpretations of Jesus' death may be retraumatizing for abuse survivors, other interpretations of his death and resurrection have the potential to be empowering and foster healing for abuse survivors. More research needs to be done concerning this issue.

42. Mary Pellauer et al., "Resources for Ritual and Recuperation," in *Sexual Assault and Abuse*, ed. Mary Pellauer, Barbara Chester, Jane A. Borjajian (San Francisco: Harper and Row, 1987), 223–247. See also Procter-Smith, "Reorganizing Victimization," 429; Heggen, *Sexual Abuse in Christian Homes and Churches*; Fortune, *Sexual Violence*, 222–224.

43. Zimmerman, *Take and Make Holy*.

44. I interviewed "Lauren" during a series of interviews that totaled fifteen hours. The interviews were conducted during a two-year period (from December 2002 to February 2003).

45. Lauren explicitly employed this language of sanctification.

46. It is important for male religious leaders to be sensitive to the fact that sexual abuse survivors may have increased difficulty trusting them if they were abused by a male. For this reason, it is important for survivors to have access to women who serve as "first aides" in the community. See Mollie Brown, *Victim No More: Ministry to Survivors of Sexual Abuse* (Mystic, Conn.: Twenty-Third, 1994).

47. Zimmerman, *Take and Make Holy*, 124.

48. Ibid., vi.

49. Mollie Brown, *Victim No More*, 36–42.

50. One must proceed with caution when discussing forgiveness in the context of sexual abuse survivors, since survivors are frequently pressured by others to forgive the perpetrator and "resolve" the trauma. Marie Fortune and others who have worked closely with survivors in their process of healing stress that the process of forgiveness cannot be rushed or it results in guilt and shame, thwarting the process of recovery.

51. Fortune, "Forgiveness."

52. Brown, *Victim No More*, 45–49.

53. Rebecca Coffey, *Unspeakable Truths and Happy Endings*.

Bibliography

Allen, Jon G. *Coping with Trauma: A Guide to Self-Understanding*. Washington, D.C.: American Psychiatric Press, 1995.

Aquinas, Thomas. *Summa Theologiae*. New York: Benziger, 1948.

Armsworth, Mary, and Karin Stronck. "Intergenerational Effects of Incest on Parenting: Skills, Abilities, and Attitudes." *Journal of Counseling and Development* 77, no. 3 (1999): 303–315.

Banyard, Victoria. "The Impact of Childhood Sexual Abuse and Family Functioning on Four Dimensions of Women's Later Parenting." *Child Abuse and Neglect* 21, no. 11 (1997): 1095–1107.

Benson, Paul. "Free Agency and Self-Worth." *Journal of Philosophy* 91 (1994): 650–668.

Benson, P., and B. Spilka. "God Image as a Function of Self-Esteem and Locus of Control." *Journal for the Scientific Study of Religion* 12 (1973): 297–310.

Berger, Leslie Beth. *Incest, Work and Women: Understanding the Consequences of Incest on Women's Careers, Work and Dreams*. Springfield, Ill.: Charles C. Thomas, 1998.

The Book of Discipline of the United Methodist Church. Nashville: United Methodist Publishing House, 1996.

Bowlin, John. *Contingency and Fortune in Aquinas's Ethics*. New York: Cambridge University Press, 1999.

Briere, John. *Child Abuse Trauma: Theory and Treatment of the Lasting Effects*. Newbury Park, Calif.: Sage, 1992.

Brock, Rita. *Journeys by Heart: A Christology of Erotic Power*. New York: Crossroad, 1988.

Brock, Rita, and Joanne Carlson Brown. "For God So Loved the World?" In *Violence Against Women and Children*, ed. Carol Adams and Marie Fortune. New York: Continuum, 1995, 36–59.

Brown, Mary Crist. *Free to Believe: Liberating Images of God for Women*. Cleveland: Pilgrim Press, 2000.

Brown, Mollie. *Victim No More: Ministry of Survivors of Sexual Abuse*. Mystic, Conn.: Twenty-Third, 1994.

Browne, A., and D. Finkelhor. "Impact of Child Sexual Abuse: A Review of the Research." *Psychological Bulletin* 99 (1986): 66–77.

Bryant, S., and L. Range. "Suicidality in College Women Who Were Sexually and Physically Abused and Physically Punished by Parents." *Violence and Victims* (1995): 195–201.

Buri, J. "Psychoanalytic Bases for One's Image of God: Fact or Artifact?" Paper presented at the annual meeting of the Midwestern Psychological Association, Chicago, May 1990.

Buri, J., and R. Mueller. "Conceptions of Parents, Conceptions of Self, and Conceptions of God." Paper presented at the annual convention of the American Psychological Association, New York, May 1987.

Bussert, Joy M. K. *Battered Women from a Theology of Suffering to an Ethic of Empowerment*. New York: Kutztown, 1986.

Butler, Judith. *Bodies That Matter: On the Discursive Limits of "Sex."* New York: Routledge, 1993.

———. "Contingent Foundations." In *Feminist Contentions: A Philosophical Exchange*, ed. Seyla Benhabib et al. New York: Routledge, 1995, 35–58.

———. "For a Careful Reading." In *Feminist Contentions: A Philosophical Exchange*, ed. Seyla Benhabib et. al. New York: Routledge, 1995, 127–144.

———. *Gender Trouble: Feminism and the Subversion of Identity*. New York: Routledge, 1990.

———. "Performing Acts and Gender Constitution: An Essay in Phenomenology and Feminist Theory." In *Performing Feminisms: Feminist Critical Theory and Theatre*, ed. Sue Ellen Case. Baltimore: John Hopkins University Press, 1990, 270–282.

———. *The Psychic Life of Power: Theories in Subjection*. Stanford, Calif.: Stanford University Press, 1997.

———. "Variations on Sex and Gender." In *Feminism as Critique: Essays on the Politics of Gender in Late Capitalist Societies*, ed. Seyla Benhabib and Drucilla Cornell. Cambridge: Polity, 1987, 128–142.

Butler, Judith, Ernesto Laclau, and Slavoj Žižek. *Contingency, Hegemony, Universality: Contemporary Dialogues on the Left*. London: Versa, 2000.

Cameron, Catherine. *Resolving Childhood Trauma: A Long-Term Study of Abuse Survivors*. Thousand Oaks, Calif.: Sage, 2000.

Card, Claudia. "Oppression and Resistance: Frye's Politics of Reality." *Hypatia* 1, no. 1 (April 1986): 149–166.

———. *The Unnatural Lottery: Character and Moral Luck*. Philadelphia: Temple University Press, 1996.

Carmen, E. H., P. P. Rieker, and T. Mills. "Victims of Violence and Psychiatric Illness." *American Journal of Psychiatry* 141 (1984): 378–383.

Carr, Anne E. *The Theological Method of Karl Rahner*. Missoula, Mont.: Scholars Press, 1977.

———. "Theology and Experience in the Thought of Karl Rahner." *Journal of Religion* 53, no. 3 (July 1973): 359–376.

Casey, Keree. "Surviving Abuse: Shame, Anger, Forgiveness." *Pastoral Psychology* 46 (March 1998): 223–231.

Cashman, Hilary. *Christianity and Child Sexual Abuse*. London: Society for Promoting Christian Knowledge, 1993.

Catechism of the Catholic Church. 2nd ed. Washington. D.C.: United States Catholic Conference, 2000.

Chartier, M., and L. Goehner. "A Study of the Relationship of Parent-Adolescent Communication, Self-Esteem, and God Image." *Journal of Psychology and Theology* 4 (1976): 227–232.

Childress, James. *Who Should Decide?* Oxford: Oxford University Press, 1982.

Chu, J., and D. Dill. "Dissociative Symptoms in Relation to Child Physical and Sexual Abuse." *American Journal of Psychiatry* 147 (1990): 887–892.

Cicchetti, Dante. "How Research on Child Maltreatment Has Informed the Study of Child Development: Perspectives from Developmental Psychology." In *Child Maltreatment: Theory and Research on the Causes and Consequences of Child Abuse and Neglect*, ed. D. Cicchetti and V. Carlson. New York: Cambridge University Press, 1989, 377–431.

Cicchetti, Dante, et al. "The Emergence of the Self in Atypical Populations." In *The Self in Transition: Infancy to Childhood*, ed. D. Cicchetti and M. Beeghley. Chicago: University of Chicago Press, 1990, 309–344.

Clark, Donald. "Sexual Abuse in the Church: The Law Steps In." *The Christian Century* 110, no. 12 (April 14, 1993): 396–398.

Coffey, Rebecca. *Unspeakable Truths and Happy Endings: Human Cruelty and the New Trauma Therapy*. Lutherville, Md.: Sidran Press, 1998.

Cohen, Tamar. "Motherhood Among Incest Survivors." *Child Abuse and Neglect* 19, no. 12 (2000): 1423–1429.

Cole, Pamela M., et al. "Parenting Difficulties: Adult Survivors of Father-Daughter Incest." *Child Abuse and Neglect* 16, no. 2 (1992): 39–49.

Coons, M. M. "Child Abuse and Multiple Personality Disorder: Review of the Literature and Suggestions for Treatment." *Child Abuse and Neglect* 10, no. 4 (1986): 455–462.

Cooper-White, Pamela. *The Cry of Tamar: Violence Against Women and the Church's Response*. Philadelphia: Fortress, 1995.

Courtois, Christine A. *Healing the Incest Wound: Adult Survivors in Therapy*. New York: Norton, 1988.

Cozzens, Donald. *Sacred Silence: Denial and the Crisis in the Church*. Collegeville, Minn: Liturgical Press, 2004.

Davaney, Sheila Greeve. "Continuing the Story, but Departing the Text: A Historicist Interpretation of Feminist Norms in Theology." In *Horizons in Feminist Theology:*

Identity, Tradition, and Norms, ed. Rebecca S. Chopp and Sheila Greeve Davaney. Minneapolis: Fortress Press, 1997, 198–214.

———. "The Limits of the Appeal to Women's Experience." In *Shaping New Vision*, ed. Clarissa W. Atkinson. Ann Arbor, Mich.: VMI Research Press, 1987, 31–49.

Davidson, J. R., et al. "The Association of Sexual Assault and Attempted Suicide Within the Community." *Archives of General Psychiatry* 53 (1996): 550–555.

Dillon, Robin. "Self-Respect: Moral, Emotional, Political." *Ethics* 107 (1997): 226–249.

DiPaolo, Michael. "The Impact of Multiple Childhood Trauma on Homeless Adolescents." In *Children of Poverty: Studies on the Effects of Single Parenthood, the Feminization of Poverty, and Homelessness*, ed. Stuart Bruchey. New York: Garland, 1999.

Douglas, Anne. "Reported Anxieties Concerning Intimate Parenting in Women Sexually Abused as Children." *Child Abuse and Neglect* 24, no. 3 (2000): 425–434.

Epstein, Seymour. "Cognitive-Experiential Self Theory: Implications for Developmental Psychology." *Self Processes and Development* 23 (1991): 78–124.

Engel, Mary Potter. "Evil, Sin and Violation of the Vulnerable." In *Lift Every Voice: Constructing Christian Theology from the Underside*, ed. Mary Potter Engel. Maryknoll, N.Y.: Orbis Books, 1998, 152–164.

———. "Historical Theology and Violence Against Women." In *Violence Against Women and Children*, ed. Carol Adams and Marie Fortune. New York: Continuum, 1995, 242–261.

———. "Historical Theology and Violenge Against Women: Unearthing Popular Tradition of Just Battery." In *Revisioning the Past*, ed. Mary Potter Engel and Walter Wyman. Minneapolis: Augsburg Fortress, 1992, 51–76.

Everly, George S., Jr. "Psychotraumatology." In *Psychotraumatology: Key Papers and Core Concepts in Post-traumatic Stress*, ed. George S. Everly, Jr., and Jeffrey M. Lating. New York: Plenum Press, 1995, 3–8.

Farley, Wendy. *Tragic Vision and Divine Compassion*. Louisville, Ky.: Westminster, 1990.

Feldmeth, Joanne, and Midge Finley. *We Weep for Ourselves and Our Children: A Christian Guide for Survivors of Childhood Sexual Abuse*. San Francisco: HarperSanFrancisco, 1990.

Finkelhor, David, and A. Browne. "The Traumatic Impact of Child Sexual Abuse: A Conceptualization." *American Journal of Orthopsychiatry* 55 (1984): 530–541.

Finkelhor, David, et al. "Sexual Abuse in a National Survey of Adult Men and Women: Prevalence, Characteristics, and Risk Factors." *Child Abuse and Neglect* 14, no. 1 (1990): 19–28.

———. *Sourcebook on Child Sexual Abuse*. Newbury Park, Calif.: Sage, 1986.

Flax, Jane. *Thinking Fragments: Psychoanalysis, Feminism and Postmodernism in the Contemporary West*. Berkeley: University of California Press, 1990.

Flynn, Kathryn. *The Sexual Abuse of Women by Members of the Clergy*. Jefferson, N.C.: McFarland & Company, 2003.

Fortune, Marie M. "Forgiveness: The Last Step." In *Violence Against Women and Children: A Christian Theological Sourcebook*, ed. Carol Adams and Marie Fortune. New York: Continuum, 1995, 201–206.

———. *Is Nothing Sacred? When Sex Invades the Pastoral Relationship*. San Francisco: Harper and Row, 1989.

———. "Justice Making in the Aftermath of Woman Battering." In *Violence Against Women and Children: A Christian Theological Sourcebook*, ed. Carol Adams and Marie Fortune. New York: Continuum, 1995, 179–190.

———. "Responding to Clergy Sexual Abuse: An Interview." *Witness* 75 (1992): 15–19.

———. *Sexual Violence: The Unmentionable Sin*. New York: Pilgrim Press, 1983.

Fulkerson, Mary McClintock. "Changing the Subject: Feminist Theology and Discourse." *Literature and Theology* 10 (June 1996): 131–147.

Gilfus, Mary. "The Price of the Ticket: A Survivor-Centered Appraisal of Trauma Theory." *Violence Against Women* 5, no. 11 (1999): 1238–1258.

Gonsiorek, John C., ed. *Breach of Trust: Sexual Exploitation by Health Care Professionals and Clergy*. Thousand Oaks, Calif.: Sage, 1995.

Gothard, Bill. *Supplementary Alumni Book, Research Principles of Life*. Vol. 5. Oak Park, Ill.: Institute in Basic Youth Conflicts, 1979.

Gudorf, Christine E. *Victimization: Examining Christian Complicity*. Philadelphia: Trinity Press International, 1992.

Hall, Terese. "Spiritual Effects of Childhood Sexual Abuse in Adult Christian Women." *Journal of Psychology and Theology* 23 (1995): 129–134.

Harter, Susan. *The Construction of the Self: A Developmental Perspective*. New York: Guilford Press, 1999.

———. "The Effects of Child Abuse on the Self-System." In *Multiple Victimization of Children: Conceptual, Developmental, Research, and Treatment Issues*, ed. B. B. Robbie Rossman and Mindy S. Rosenberg. New York: Haworth Maltreatment and Trauma Press, 1998, 147–170.

Heggen, Carolyn Holderread. *Sexual Abuse in Christian Homes and Churches*. Scottdale, Pa.: Herald Press, 1993.

Herman, Judith Lewis. "Complex PTSD: A Syndrome in Survivors of Prolonged and Repeated Trauma." In *Psychotraumatology: Key Papers and Core Concepts in Post-traumatic Stress*, ed. George S. Everly, Jr., and Jeffrey M. Lating. New York: Plenum Press, 1995, 87–102.

———. *Father-Daughter Incest*. Cambridge, Mass.: Harvard University Press, 1981.

———. *Trauma and Recovery*. New York: Basic Books, 1992.

Imbens, Annie, and Ineke Jonker. *Christianity and Incest*. Minneapolis: Fortress Press, 1992.

Isley, Paul. "Child Sexual Abuse and the Catholic Church: An Historical and Contemporary Review." *Pastoral Psychology* 45, no. 4 (1997): 277–299.

Jackson, Timothy. "Arminian Edification: Kierkegaard on Grace and Free Will." In *The Cambridge Companion to Kierkegaard*, ed. Alastair Hannay and Gordon D. Marino. Cambridge: Cambridge University Press, 1998, 235–256.

Janoff-Bulman, Ronnie. *Shattered Assumptions*. New York: Free Press, 1992.

John Jay College of Criminal Justice. *The Nature and Scope of the Problem of Sexual Abuse of Minors by Catholic Priests and Deacons in the United States*. Washington, D.C.: United States Conference of Catholic Bishops, 2004.

Justice, William, and Warren Lambert. "A Comparative Study of the Language People Use to Describe the Personalities of God and Their Earthly Parents." *Journal of Pastoral Care* 40, no. 2 (1986): 166–172.

Kane, Donna. "Perception of God by Survivors of Childhood Sexual Abuse: An Exploratory Study in an Underresearched Area." *Journal of Psychology and Theology* 21 (1993): 228–237.

Kendall-Tackett, K., et al. "Impact of Sexual Abuse on Children: A Review and Synthesis of Recent Empirical Studies." *Psychological Bulletin* 113 (1993): 164–180.

Kerins, Jacinta. "The Matter at Hand: Butler, Ontology, and the Natural Sciences." *Australian Feminist Studies* 14, no. 29 (1999): 91–104.

Keshgegian, Flora. *Redeeming Memories*. Nashville, Tenn.: Abingdon Press, 2000.

Kierkegaard, Søren. *The Journals of Søren Kierkegaard*. Trans. Alexander Dru. London: Oxford University Press, 1959.

Kleber, Rolf J., Charles R. Figley, and Berthold P. R. Gersons, eds. *Beyond Trauma: Cultural and Societal Dynamics*. New York: Plenum Press, 1995.

Koenig, Linda J., ed. *From Child Sexual Abuse to Adult Sexual Risk: Trauma, Revictimization, and Intervention*. Washington, D.C.: American Psychological Association, 2004.

Krahé, Barbara. "Child Sexual Abuse and Revictimization in Adolescence and Adulthood." In *Post-traumatic Stress Theory*, ed. Jon Harvey and Brian Pauwels. Philadelphia: Brunner/Mazel, 2000, 49–66.

Kreklewetz, C., and C. Piotrowski. "Incest Survivor Mothers: Protecting the Next Generation." *Child Abuse and Neglect* 22, no. 12 (1998): 1305–1312.

Lemoncelli, John, and Andrew Carey. "The Psychospiritual Dynamics of Adult Survivors of Abuse." *Counseling and Values* 40 (1996): 175–185.

Lerner, M. J. *The Belief in a Just World*. New York: Plenum Press, 1989.

Linnane, Brian F. "Celibacy and Sexual Malpractice: Dimensions of Power and Powerlessness in Patriarchal Society." In *Theology and the New Histories*, ed. Gary Macy. Maryknoll, N.Y.: Orbis, 1999, 227–244.

Maltz, W., and B. Holman. *Incest and Sexuality: A Guide to Understanding and Healing*. Lexington, Mass.: Lexington Books, 1987.

Manlowe, Jennifer L. *Faith Born of Seduction: Sexual Trauma, Body Image, and Religion*. New York: New York University Press, 1995.

McFarlane, Alexander C. "The Severity of Trauma." In Kleber et al., *Beyond Trauma*, 31–54.

McFarlane, Alexander C., and Bessel A. van der Kolk. "Trauma and Its Challenge to Society." In van der Kolk et al., *Traumatic Stress*, 24–46.

Means, J. Jeffrey. *Trauma and Evil: Healing the Wounded Soul*. Minneapolis: Fortress Press, 2000.

Meyers, Diana T. "Personal Autonomy or the Deconstructed Subject? A Reply to Heckman." *Hypatia* 7, no. 1 (winter 1992): 125.

———. *Self, Society, and Personal Choice.* New York: Columbia University Press, 1989.

Mills, Catherine. "Efficacy and Vulnerability: Judith Butler on Reiteration and Resistance." *Australian Feminist Studies* 15, no. 32 (2000): 271–277.

Najavits, Lisa M. "Assessment of Trauma, PTSD, and Substance Use Disorder: A Practical Guide." In *Assessing Psychological Trauma and PTSD*, ed. John P. Wilson and Terence M. Keane. New York: Guilford Press, 2004, 466–491.

———. *Seeking Safety: A Treatment Manual for PTSD and Substance Abuse.* New York: Guilford Press, 2002.

National Review Board for the Protection of Children and Young People. *A Report on the Crisis in the Catholic Church in the United States.* Washington, D.C.: United States Conference of Catholic Bishops, 2004.

Nelson, Lise. "Bodies (and Spaces) Do Matter: The Limits of Performativity." *Gender, Place and Culture* 6 (1999): 331–354.

Neuhaus, Richard John. "When Shepherds Go Astray." *First Things* 29 (1993): 55–58.

Oates, R., et al. "Prior Sexual Abuse in Mothers of Sexually Abused Children." *Child Abuse and Neglect* 22, no. 11 (1998): 1113–1118.

Office of Child and Youth Protection. *Executive Summary, Compliance Audits, Analysis of the Findings, and Recommendations.* Washington, D.C.: United States Conference of Catholic Bishops, 2004.

———. *Report on the Implementation of the Charter for the Protection of Children and Young People* (Washington, D.C.: United States Conference of Catholic Bishops, 2005).

Outka, Gene. *Agape: An Ethical Analysis.* New Haven, Conn.: Yale University Press, 1972.

———. "Equality and Individuality: Thoughts on Two Themes in Kierkegaard." *Journal of Religious Ethics* 10, no. 2 (1982): 171–203.

———. "Equality and the Fate of Theism in Modern Culture." *Journal of Religion* 67, no. 3 (1987): 275–288.

———. "On Harming Others." *Interpretation* 34, no. 4 (October 1980): 381–393.

Pellauer, Mary. "Conversation on Grace and Healing." In *Lift Every Voice: Constructing Christian Theology from the Underside*, ed. Susan B. Thistlethwaite and Mary P. Engel. Maryknoll: Orbis Books, 1998, 169–185.

———. "Resources for Ritual and Recuperation." In *Sexual Assault and Abuse*, ed. Mary Pellauer, Barbara Chester, and Jane A. Borjajian. San Francisco: Harper and Row, 1987, 223–247.

Peters, D., and L. Range. "Childhood Sexual Abuse and Current Suicidality in College Women and Men." *Child Abuse and Neglect* 19, no. 3 (1995): 335–341.

Poling, Nancy, ed. *Victim to Survivor: Women Recovering from Sexual Abuse.* Cleveland: United Church Press, 1999.

Proctor-Smith, Marjorie. "Reorganizing Victimization." In *Violence Against Women and Children*, ed. Carol Adams and Marie Fortune. New York: Continuum, 1995, 428–443.

Psalter Hymnal: Doctrinal Standards and Liturgy of the Christian Reformed Church. Grand Rapids, Mich.: Publication Committee of the Christian Reformed Church, 1959.

Rahner, Karl. "Christian Dying." In *Theological Investigations,* vol. 18. London: Darton, Longman and Todd, 1983, 226–256.

———. *The Church and the Sacraments.* Trans. W. J. O'Hara. New York: Herder and Herder, 1963.

———. "The Church's Commission to Bring Salvation and the Humanization of the World." In *Theological Investigations,* vol. 14. London: Darton, Longman and Todd, 1976, 295–313.

———. "The Comfort of Time." In *Theological Investigations,* vol. 3. London: Darton, Longman and Todd, 1967, 141–160.

———. "The 'Commandment' of Love in Relation to the Other Commandments." In *Theological Investigations,* vol. 5. London: Darton, Longman and Todd, 1966, 439–459.

———. "The Concept of Mystery in Catholic Theology." In *Theological Investigations,* vol. 4. London: Darton, Longman, and Todd, 1966, 36–76.

———. "Concerning the Relationship between Nature and Grace." In *Theological Investigations,* vol. 1. London: Darton, Longman and Todd, 1961, 297–319.

———. "The Current Relationship between Philosophy and Theology." In *Theological Investigations,* vol. 13. New York: Seabury, 1975, 61–79.

———. "The Dignity and Freedom of Man." In *Theological Investigations,* vol. 2. London: Darton, Longman and Todd, 1963, 235–264.

———. *Foundations of Christian Faith: An Introduction to the Idea of Christianity.* Trans. William V. Dych. New York: Crossroad, 1978.

———. "Grace." In *Encyclopedia of Theology: The Concise Sacramentum Mundi,* ed. Karl Rahner. London: Burns and Oates, 1975, 584–598.

———. *Grace in Freedom.* Trans. Hilda Graef. New York: Herder and Herder, 1969.

———. *Hearers of the Word.* Trans. by Michael Richards. New York: Herder and Herder, 1969.

———. *I Remember: An Autobiographical Interview with Meinhold Krauss.* Trans. Harvey D. Egan. New York: Crossroad, 1985.

———. "The Liberty of the Sick, Theologically Considered." In *Theological Investigations,* vol. 17. London: Darton, Longman and Todd, 1981, 100–113.

———. *The Love of Jesus and the Love of Neighbor,* trans. Robert Barr. New York: Crossroads, 1983.

———. *Meditations of Freedom and the Spirit.* New York: Seabury Press, 1976.

———. *On the Theology of Death.* Trans. Charles H. Henkey. New York: Herder and Herder, 1961.

———. "On the Theology of the Council." In *Theological Investigations,* vol. 5. London: Darton, Longman and Todd, 1966, 244–267.

———. "Purgatory." In *Theological Investigations,* vol. 19. New York: Crossroad, 1983, 181–193.

———. "Reflections on the Experience of Grace." In *Theological Investigations,* vol. 3. London: Darton, Longman and Todd, 1967, 86–90.

———. "Reflections on Methodology in Theology." In *Theological Investigations,* vol. 11. New York: Seabury, 1974, 68–114.
———. "Reflections on the Unity of the Love of Neighbor and the Love of God." In *Theological Investigations,* vol. 6. London: Darton, Longman and Todd, 1969, 231–249.
———. "Religious Enthusiasm and the Experience of Grace." In *Theological Investigations,* vol. 16. London: Darton, Longman, and Todd, 1979, 35–51.
———. "Religious Feeling Inside and Outside the Church." In *Theological Investigations,* vol. 17. New York: Crossroad, 1981, 228–242.
———. *Spirit in the World.* Trans. William Dych. London: Sheed and Ward, 1968.
———. "The Theological Concept of Concupiscentia." In *Theological Investigations,* vol. 1. London: Darton, Longman and Todd, 1961, 347–382.
———. "Theology of Freedom." In *Theological Investigations,* vol. 6. London: Darton, Longman and Todd, 1969, 178–196.
———. *Theology of Pastoral Action.* Trans. W. J. O'Hara. New York: Herder and Herder, 1968.
———. "The Theology of Power." In *Theological Investigations,* vol. 4. London: Darton, Longman and Todd, 1966, 391–409.
———. "Why Does God Allow Us to Suffer?" In *Theological Investigations,* vol. 19. London: Darton, Longman and Todd, 1983, 194–208.
Rediger, G. Lloyd. *Ministry and Sexuality.* Minneapolis: Fortress Press, 1990.
Root, Maria. "Reconstructing the Impact of Trauma on Personality." In *Personality and Psychopathology.* New York: Guilford Press, 1992, 229–266.
Rossetti, Stephen. "The Impact of Child Sexual Abuse on Attitudes toward God and the Catholic Church." *Child Abuse and Neglect* 19, no. 12 (1995): 1469–1481.
———. *Tragic Grace: The Catholic Church and Child Sexual Abuse.* Collegeville, Minn.: Liturgical Press, 1996.
Ruether, Rosemary Radford. "The Western Religious Tradition and Violenge Against Women in the Home." In *Christianity: Patriarchy, and Abuse: A Feminist Critique,* ed. Joanne Carlson Brown and Carole R. Bohn. New York: Pilgrim Press, 1989, 31–41.
Ruscio, Ayelet. "Predicting the Child-Rearing Practices of Mothers Sexually Abused in Childhood." *Child Abuse and Neglect* 25, no. 3 (2001): 369–387.
Russell, Diana E. H. "Incestuous Abuse of Females." In Kleber, Figley, and Gersons, *Beyond Trauma,* 171–186.
———. *The Secret Trauma: Incest in the Lives of Girls and Women.* New York: Basic Books, 1986.
Russell, Diana E. H., and Rebecca M. Bolen. *The Epidemic of Rape and Child Sexual Abuse in the United States.* Thousand Oaks, Calif.: Sage, 2000.
Scarry, Elaine. *The Body in Pain: The Making and Unmaking of the World.* New York: Oxford University Press, 1985.
Schene, P. "Child Abuse and Neglect Policy, History, Models, and Future Directions." In *The APSAC Handbook of Child Maltreatment,* ed. John Briere et al. Thousand Oaks: Sage, 1996, 385–397.

Selected Theological Statements of the Presbyterian Church. Louisville, Ky.: Presbyterian Church (USA) Office of Theology and Worship, 1998.

Sheinberg, Marsha, and Peter Fraenkel. *The Relational Trauma of Incest.* New York: Guilford Press, 2001.

Shupe, Anson D., ed. *Wolves Within the Fold.* New Brunswick, N.J.: Rutgers University Press, 1998.

Silbert, M., and A. Pines. "Sexual Child Abuse as an Antecedent to Prostitution." *Bulletin of the Menninger Clinic* 5, no. 4 (1981): 428–438.

Soelle, Dorothee. *Suffering.* Philadelphia: Fortress Press, 1975.

Stepakoff, S. "Effects of Sexual Victimization on Suicidal Ideation and Behavior in U.S. College Women." *Suicide and Life-Threatening Behavior* 28, no. 1 (1998): 107–126.

Stern, Daniel N. *The Interpersonal World of the Infant: A View from Psychoanalysis and Developmental Psychology.* New York: Basic Books, 1985.

Suchocki, Marjorie Hewitt. *The Fall to Violence.* New York: Continuum, 1994.

Summerfield, Derek. "Addressing Human Response to War and Atrocity: Major Challenges in Research and Practices and the Limitations of Western Psychiatric Methods." In Kleber, Figley, and Gersons, *Beyond Trauma,* 17–29.

Terr, Lenore C. "Childhood Traumas: An Outline and Overview." *American Journal of Psychiatry* 148, no. 1 (1991): 10–20.

Todd, Shelley. "An Exploration of the Concept of God Espoused by Female Adult Survivors of Sexual Abuse." Ph.D. diss., New Orleans Baptist Theological Seminary, 1991.

Torre, Lilliam. "Predictors of the Concept of God in a Sample of Adult Survivors of Father-Daughter Incest." Ph.D. diss., University of Miami, 1993.

Tracy, Steven. "Sexual Abuse and Forgiveness." *Journal of Psychology and Theology* 27, no. 3 (1999): 219–229.

Turell, Susan, and Mary Armsworth. "Differentiating Incest Survivors Who Self-Mutilate." *Child Abuse and Neglect* 24, no. 2 (2000): 237–249.

van der Kolk, Bessel A., and Alexander C. McFarlane. "The Black Hole of Trauma." In van der Kolk et al., *Traumatic Stress,* 3–23.

———. "The Body Keeps the Score: Approaches to the Psychobiology of Posttraumatic Stress Disorder." In van der Kolk et al., *Traumatic Stress,* 214–241.

———. "The Complexity of Adaptation to Trauma." In van der Kolk et al., *Traumatic Stress,* 182–213.

———. "A General Approach to Treatment of Posttraumatic Stress Disorder." In van der Kolk et al., *Traumatic Stress,* 417–440.

———. "History of Trauma in Psychiatry." In van der Kolk et al., *Traumatic Stress,* 47–74.

———. "Trauma and Memory." In van der Kolk et al., *Traumatic Stress,* 279–302.

van der Kolk, Bessel A., Alexander C. McFarlane, and Lars Weisaeth, eds. *Traumatic Stress: The Effects of Overwhelming Experience on Mind, Body, and Society.* New York: Guilford Press, 1996.

van der Kolk, Bessel A., Onno van der Hart, and Charles R. Marmar. "Dissociation and Information Processing in Posttraumatic Stress Disorder." In van der Kolk et al., *Traumatic Stress*, 303–327.

Vasterling, Veronica. "Butler's Sophisticated Contructivism: A Critical Assessment." *Hypatia* 14, no. 3 (1999): 17–38.

Waites, Elizabeth. *Trauma and Survival: Post-traumatic and Dissociative Disorders in Women*. New York: Norton, 1993.

Williams, Linda. "Recall of Childhood Trauma: A Prospective Study of Women's Memories of Child Sexual Abuse." *Journal of Consulting and Clinical Psychology* 62, no. 6 (1994): 1167–1176.

Weedon, Chris. *Feminist Practice and Poststructuralist Theory*. Oxford: Blackwell, 1987.

Weems, Renita J. *Battered Love: Marriage, Sex, and Violence in the Hebrew Prophets*. Minneapolis: Fortress Press, 1995.

Weil, Simone. *Waiting for God*. New York: Harper and Row, 1951.

Westerlund, Elaine. *Women's Sexuality after Childhood Incest*. New York: Norton, 1992.

Young, Leslie. "Sexual Abuse and the Problem of Embodiment." *Child Abuse and Neglect* 16, no. 1 (1992): 89–100.

Zimmerman, Mari West. *Take and Make Holy: Honoring the Sacred in the Healing Journey of Abuse Survivors*. Chicago: Liturgy Training, 1995.

Zuravin, S., et al. "The Intergenerational Cycle of Child Maltreatment: Continuity vs. Discontinuity." *Journal of Interpersonal Violence* 11, no. 3 (1996): 15–34.

Index